MARY CARBERY'S
WEST CORK JOURNAL

1898–1901

MARY CARBERY'S WEST CORK JOURNAL

1898–1901

or

"From the Back of Beyond"

EDITED BY JEREMY SANDFORD

THE LILLIPUT PRESS

First published 1998 by
THE LILLIPUT PRESS LTD
62–63 Sitric Road, Arbour Hill,
Dublin 7, Ireland.

A CIP record for this title is available from the British Library.

ISBN 1 874675 36 8

*The Lilliput Press receives financial assistance from
An Chomhairle Ealaíon / The Arts Council of Ireland.*

*The Lilliput Press is grateful to Valerie Pakenham for her editorial assistance
in the preparation of this book.*

Set in 10.5 on 14 Sabon with display headings and folios in Felix Titling
and designed by Elizabeth van Amerongen
Printed and bound in England by MPG Books of Cornwall

CONTENTS

ILLUSTRATIONS

INTRODUCTION

WHEN MY GRANDMOTHER, as a young woman over a hundred years ago, married Algernon, the 9th Lord Carbery, he took her to his neo-medieval castle on the south-west seaboard of County Cork.

His family claimed descent from Elystan Glodrydd, Prince of Fferlys, and the name of the castle was Castle Freke. Mary Carbery went out to West Cork from England unsuspecting that she would be so overwhelmed by its beauty. But at once she fell for it entirely.

Of her first days and her great happiness there she has left little record. But as a boy I used to sit with her at my parents' home while she described the early days to me. She used to say that since she had left the castle she'd been a wanderer all her life. She consoled herself in her latter days by writing books. But her heart rested still in the past. Although it wasn't until much later that I learnt the whole story, even then, in my mind, a fairytale quality attached itself to the castle.

Grandmother's happiness was short-lived. A few years after their marriage Algernon began to sicken with consumption. Within a painfully short time he was dead. My grandmother, then in her early thirties, was left as sole mistress of this many-towered place on its hilly promontory above Ounahincha Bay, and of its many acres of woodland, moor and marsh, and of the "holy" lake of Kilkerran. Offshore the sea was studded with the islands, mostly desolate but some inhabited, still known as "Carbery's Hundred Islands".

7

A few years back I visited Castle Freke, and I found it every bit as marvellous as she'd described it. Here was the little market town of Ross Carbery, with its brightly painted houses, many of them pubs, and the grey streets that seemed too wide for them. Here was the sea tearing at the Long Strand, with the tall Atlantic waters breaking over it in foam, here the mantling woods, the sandhills and the bogs, the long drive skirting the grey marsh. And then, amidst deep woods, on a sudden eminence, with its Wagnerian terraces falling from it southward and westward towards the sea, and its many towers standing up against the sky, the castle, more beautiful than anything I could have dreamed.

As I drew nearer I saw that the face of the castle was blank, its towers shattered, and its windows empty. But this did not diminish its grandeur. Still it stood up, as romantic a sight as I had ever seen.

At the West Lodge I found someone waiting for me. It was a resident of the village, whose father had worked for my grandmother, and who himself later became steward of the ruined estate.

Knocked – knocked – ah sir, all knocked. I'll tell YOU now, if 'twas up today, wouldn't be allowed to do it. Ah sir, and now if you walk with me yonder, you can see it. There sir stood the castle. And there were the doors of cedar and pillars all of marble. I'll tell you now. Yonder the bedroom of her Ladyship, and there the boudoir with the great view of the ocean. And from here you can see well nigh all the Carbery lands and demesne, the bog and the woodland, and pasture, all knocked now, all gone back.

She was far younger than you sir when she was mistress of it all. And here after her Lord had died she lived alone ... I have heard that her family desired her to return to England. But she did not leave.

What were the feelings of this young woman in her castle amidst the bogs and woodland, with her husband's ashes buried beneath the headland where she was to erect a huge cross by the sea? From other villagers I heard other stories; how she would ride endlessly the empty countryside. I thought I could fancy something of her strange solitude. Later, in the attic of Eye Manor in Herefordshire, Mary Carbery's final home, I unexpectedly came upon her journal.

MARY CARBERY was not the first woman to write of the joys and tribulations of running that ill-fated estate. In the seventeenth century, then called Rathbarry, it had formed much of the backdrop for the diaries of Elizabeth Freke (1641–1714), sub-titled "Some Few Remembrances of my Misfortuns which have attended me in my unhappy life since I were marryed: whc was November the 14, 1671"; the diaries were edited by Mary and published in Cork in 1913. Freke, later Evans-Freke, was the family name of the Carberys. Elizabeth was another young Englishwoman, who came out as an Irishman's bride in 1676, returning eventually in 1696; Rathbarry Castle had been bought by Captain Arthur Freke, her uncle, from Lord Barrymore, son-in-law of Richard Boyle, 1st Earl of Cork, who had "founded" Clonakilty in 1605 and settled it with a hundred Protestant English families.

Other writers too have celebrated this beautiful area of West Cork and have acquainted us with that lost world in which, as Gifford Lewis writes in her introduction to *The Selected Letters of Somerville and Ross*, "it is eventually borne in upon the reader that in the Anglo-Irish 'ascendancy' of the end of the nineteenth century and the beginning of the twentieth was an enormous confidence trick, shored up by faithful servants and good horsemanship".

"Let us take Carbery and grind its bones to make our bread," wrote Edith Somerville, Mary's well-known literary neighbour, to Violet Martin, a.k.a. Martin Ross. The administrative district of Carbery formed the location for *Some Experiences of an Irish R.M.* and other works of Somerville and Ross. Drishane, Edith Somerville's family home, was in Castletownshend, a few miles up the coast. She rode with the West Carbery Hunt. One letter tells how her sister, Hildegarde Somerville, went to a dance at Castle Freke in July 1905 and

arrived … this morning at 6.30. She then went to bed … She says it was an excellent dance. Crowds of surplus men, perfect floor, band, supper, champagne – Lady C. had ordered an army of assistant hireling waiters from Cork, & every man of them arrived blind drunk & had to be put to bed instantly! However all went well. H.'s young charges, from Edie Whitla to Loo Loo, got on first rate & had all the dancing they wanted, & H. herself said that it was very good fun. There were some very wild Easterns there – Nevill Penrose heard a man say to the girl of his heart "Blasht yer soul, where were ye hiding that I couldn't find ye!" But all the decent people were there too; the incredibly kind Mrs Guinness had lent Bock a most lovely dress. *Hand painted chiffon* and silver spangles, H. says it must have cost about 20 guineas.

Mary's journal, hitherto unpublished, gives further glimpses into this world when most of these people had little inkling that, within very few years, much of Ireland would be independent of England; or that Castle Freke estate and the employment of the many people who worked there would so soon be a thing of the past.

"IF QUEEN VICTORIA can learn Hindustani then I can learn Irish," Mary wrote. She became entranced by the customs and history of Ireland.

She had been born in England in 1867 into the Toulmin family who lived in Childwickbury, between St Albans and Harpenden, and later at The Pré, near St Albans. She describes life up to the age of seventeen in her book *Happy World*, started when she was twelve but not finished until she was living in a cottage at my father's home in 1941. Her grandfather had made a small fortune with his fleet of merchant ships. Her father preferred a life of worthy leisure with his wife and many children in the country.

Mary's childhood included visits to local poor or sick, and to prisoners in St Albans Gaol. At one point in she falls sick and apparently nearly dies. "'You were unconscious, to the world,' her mother says. 'You seemed very happy. Now and then you tried to beat time with your hand. I thought you were dying. I thought you were listening to angelic music ...'" This experience led Mary to wonder if she had a musical talent. Her sister Connie in *her* book *Happy Memories*, describes how she "attended the Royal Academy of Music in London, and later won the silver medal. ... At St Albans she helped to found the School of Music, and took a great interest in the Abbey choir-boys, to one of whom she gave piano lessons in The Pré and he went on to become a great organist."

At the end of *Happy World* Mary appears to be a little in love with her cousin, Hugh Beaufort. At a garden party he asks her, " 'I suppose you're too old to come up a tree for a talk? You couldn't in that frock? What a pity! I want to ask you something. Mary ...'

'You're wanted, sir, to make up a set,' said the butler, and off Hugh went, full tilt, with a cloud on his usually sunny face."

Her sister Connie wrote, "I have heard it said she was 'the most beautiful girl in Hertfordshire'." In 1890, at a May Ball in Cambridge, Mary met the man who was to be her husband. In November of that year they were married.

Mary and Algy passed through Folkestone on their honeymoon and later lived for a period in a villa at El Bior, above Algiers, where the climate was thought to be better for Algy's already failing health. At that time, so we learn from a reminiscence in Mary's journal, she was expecting her first baby. This was John, born in 1892.

In 1897 her second son, Ralfe, was born. Algy was by now very ill. In the journal we encounter a memory of him at this time, lying in a tent, possibly a small open-sided marquee, on the lawn.

Algy died in the Imperial Hotel in the Malvern Hills in England in 1898, having travelled there in the belief that the climate there might secure him a few more weeks of life. The six-year-old John ("Jacky") became the new Lord Carbery. Mary was to be mistress of the castle and estate until John came of age. This is the point at which her journal begins.

THE PEOPLE OF CASTLE FREKE

In the House
Mary, Lady Carbery (*aet.* 30–33); John ("Jacky"), Lord Carbery (*aet.* 6–9); "Baby", Ralfe Evans-Freke (*aet.* 1–3); Miss Singer, nanny; Miss D., governess; Mr H. Perry-Ayscough, tutor; Taylor, Scottish maid; Court, housekeeper; Ellen, Alice, Annie, Nancy, Julia, and other maids; Amy, nursery maid; Carmody, butler; Mrs Carmody and Alice in the West Lodge; Thomas Ward and Charles de Courcy, footmen; Ned Good, odd man.

In the Garden
Jenkins, head gardener; Mrs Jenkins and Victor and Dennis, little boys; Hayes; Paddy Regan; Robert Brien, an old soldier known as "her ladyship's own gardening man"; Jerry Spillane; Mr and Mrs Duggan.

In the Stables
Nobbs, a young English coachman; James McCarthy, groom; Jerome and Jack, his brothers, helpers; Con Brien, helper, later chauffeur.

Keeper
Hay, Mrs Hay, and children.

On the Farm
Mr M. and Mr Duthie, successive stewards; Gaucher, cowman; Curly Collins, carter; Mike Madden, labourer; Mrs Leary, a lunatic; Leary; Hawkins and Mrs Hawkins, lodge-keepers (parents of Alice and Annie); Con Brien, watcher of the strand; three roadmen, including Paddy Spillane; old Mike; Mrs Leary, fisherwoman; Johnny Sweeney, fisherman; Costello, carpenter.

SPRING

Si nostre vie est moins qu'une journée
En l'éternel, si l'an qui faict le tour
Chasse noz jours sans espoir de retour,
Si perissable est toute chose née.

Que songes-tu, mon âme emprisonée?
Pourquoy te plaist l'obscur de nostre jour,
Si pour voler en un plus cler sejour
Tu as au dos l'aele bien empanée?

Là est le bien que tout esprit desire,
Là, le repos ou tout le monde aspire,
Là est l'amour, là, le plaisir encore.

Là, o mon âme, au plus hault ciel guidée,
Tu y pourras recongnoistre l'Idée
De la beauté, qu'en ce monde j'adore.

Joachim du Bellay (1525–60), *Sonnets ii*

CASTLE FREKE is an earthly paradise. It stands at the top of a hill overlooking the Atlantic. Croachna, a green hill, separates south and west views, Galley Head is the boundary to the south. On the west, beyond a beautiful line of miles of coast, the pointed Stags (rocks) shut in the world. The next parish, the people say, is America. But in between the old world and the new lies the mystic island of Moy Mell, land of happy departed spirits, to be seen on clear days by the eye of faith. At night a moonlit path leads thither.

Our shore is partly sand hills, grey with marram grass, partly high cliffs, covered with heather and thrift and short grass where rabbits and puffins live amicably together. Seabirds add to the wild solitude, plover cry mournfully over Ounahincha Bog with its silver stream and its ancient cliffs, the coastline of a thousand years ago. Tiny farms and cabins lie between brakes of gorse and bracken; bo'reens (lanes) creep about the hills, their surface often raised and rocky. At the south end of the long strand is the Battery, a collection of fishermen's cabins. Here, and all around us, live the dear people known as *the neighbours*, from whom I have received, with deep gratitude, unfailing affection, and who are a constant source of concern and delight.

My bedroom faces south. From my bed I see the Galley Head whose intermittent light flashes round the walls at night. I look over the sea and the Dulig Rock at whose deep foot lies a Spanish galleon, a ship laden with silver ducats, and who knows how many more hulks? I see the sandhills, and Croachna dotted with sheep and cattle.

I look down upon the tree-tops in the wood, which in Spring make a garden of bronze, pink, green and amber. Through the two wide-opened windows comes the South Wind with his freshness and scents, carrying the soft booming waves on the Long Strand.

At night the outlook is mysterious and beautiful; the shadowy woods, the moonlit sea, the Galley light and, rarely, small pricks of light from a passing ship.

These are my earliest and latest ejaculations:

"Praised be Thou, O my Lord, of Brother Wind and the air, and of the clouds and the clear, and of all the times of the sky whereby Thou dost make provision for Thy creatures.

"Praised be Thou, O my Lord, of Sister Moon and the stars that Thou hast shapen in the heavens, bright and precious and comely."

TODAY I went to see Mrs Patrick Donovan. Her little girl Mary-Ellen has grown "distant in her mind", which means hysterical. I am to take her to the "Children's Hospitable" when next I go to Cork.

"'Tis fallin' away the poor child is this last two months, and she once a fine lump of a girl."

Mary-Ellen is only seven; a pretty little creature with blue eyes and shadows under them. She is terribly thin, arms like little sticks show through her ragged sleeves. She cries when she hears she is to go to Cork. "No then! No," and clutches her mother's hand.

"Och then, there's worse happened us than that," Mrs Donovan continues volubly, "since ye was last here the ould cow died on us, and the little boneens (pigs), they died on us for want of the milk ... an' the harse ..."

"You've still got the horse, I hope!"

"Och then, we have a sart of a harse, but the doonkey ..."

"Surely nothing has happened to the donkey?"

"Sure then 'twas ould and weak, an' last Sunday we left it to go to Mass an' when we got back it was lyin' acrost the door ..."

"It hadn't, surely it hadn't ..."

"It had so. It had died on us, God help us!"

Poor creatures! Their farm is too small to keep them after they have paid their rent. The potatoes last year were diseased. The animals died of starvation. If they were to be given a cow today, they would have to sell it tomorrow to pay the rent. Their landlord is an English absentee and cares nothing for the people. "He have the hard heart," they say, "or he'd come to see what way it is wid us all."

The days are very full with many Poor Things coming to the house with their bundles of troubles. The little I can do to help them seems a drop in the ocean. They are desperately poor and feckless. Also they are wonderfully patient. When I am out they wait for hours to see me.

The threstill with her warblynge.

I heard it through a dream at dawn, and waking, went to a north window to hear the chorus rising from the trees on the edge of the wood. Throstle, mavis, ouzel-cock; or thrush, missel-thrush and blackbird – spraying the air with jewels of song ...

Dear God, I thank Thee that I can hear them; that I am not too deaf to hear them.

FORTY CHIMNEYS have to be swept after winter's fires, all of them are high and some are very twisty. The old Clonakilty sweep who contended with them for a lifetime has died and his son does not feel competent to carry on the work. So we have bought a set of sweep's brooms, jointed like fishing rods. Duthie has chosen Mike Twomey to be the sweep. His workfellows jeer and wonder how he can so demean himself. When they hear that he will be paid sixpence a chimney over and above his wage, they all want to be sweeps.

TODAY I have been visiting Miss Regan, a dress-maker, strange though that seems in so small and poor a place. She is a delicate little creature, yet she plods along, living by herself in a two-roomed house.

Her father was a soldier. "This day", she told me, "is the anniversary of the day when the Crimean War was over and peace declared, when every soldier became a hero." Her father was a hero too, and "the night he came home to Ross he knew it". I suppose she meant there was much "drink taken".

The Crimean War is a reality to her, but to me Balaclava and Alma are as remote as Waterloo or Trafalgar. I remember hearing that my grandfather's ships – fine sailing ships they were – carried stores of all kinds for the troops. When I told Miss Regan this we seemed at once to become relations. How delightful that my grandfather's ships carried food and boots and warm clothes for her father.

She was making a coat of thick frieze, woven by Hayes the weaver. " 'Twill never wear out," she said, stroking it with her thin fingers, "some person will be wearin' it when we are all in our coffins, *God help us*!"

WE ARE HIDDEN in a sea fog as chickens under the hen's feathers. Angel Gabriel himself could not find us. For all we know, the sea may be coming up and up on the land, filling its channels of a thousand years ago, so that when the fog has lifted we may see waves leaping on the ancient cliffs on the eastern side of Ounahincha, the tide racing between us and Croachna, sweeping up the glen, joining Rahavarrig to Kilkerran, making the hilly fields, still known by their ancient names of Great Island and Little Island, true islands once more.

What a delicious surprise! What April fools we! The sea throwing up his head and roaring with laughter and we with him!

Or supposing, under cover of the fog, this hill on which we live has come loose and is now floating into the west, so that tomorrow may see us sister island to Moy Mell!

ONE OF THE RARER joys – to look down on the tops of trees. The small leaves have broken from the purple and red buds of yesterday; all through the soft night they were pressing and straining against the sheath that held them. The garden of the tree-tops is today of amazing beauty. In a day or two the rose, primrose and bronze tenderness will be green, the incredible green of Spring, bright on the boughs of lichened and weather-beaten trees.

CASTLE FREKE is so beautiful that one grudges every moment spent away from it. One of its charms is its distance from other big houses, whose owners otherwise would constantly be descending on it with a gang of guests who would over-run the place and talk worldly talk, ask questions and go back and say things.

Isolation means a deeper love and sense – not of possession, but of being a part of something essential in the Great Scheme of Beauty and Life.

I can imagine, if I had to go to London in Spring, returning if it were possible by the next day's mail.

THE RAIN is coming down, not in drops, but in rods infinitely fine. Imagine if God sent a cold blast and froze the rods into millions of thread-like icicles reaching from Heaven to Earth, and then suppose a low sun shone out. That would be something wonderful and gorgeous in its radiance and colour; something "new under the sun" that would astonish and dumbfounder the vexed spirit of the Preacher. And then suppose that suddenly the wind set every ice-thread shaking and humming, making the strangest sound ever heard between earth and sky. What would the Preacher say then?

The primroses stand on their hairy pink legs, holding each its cup of rain. The bluebells are more easily daunted, dear feminine things; they droop their wet ringlets towards the earth, and look dilapidated.

Rain, rain! The bees are having a long Lent; there is no nectar in the sodden flowers. Jenkins feeds them with syrup. Doubtless the youngest bees, born under weeping skies, think this is the best that God can do! How little they know!

Today I met a bee whose basket was full of whitey-green pollen instead of the usual gold or brown. Jenkins, that great bee-man, believes the bee had been on the blackberry patch near the keeper's house. He says a bee never mixes pollens. If she begins the day on blackberry she will stick to that until evening.

I like to linger beside the hives to watch the little harvesters coming in with their loads of gold from dandelion, of pale yellow from apple blossom, brown from gorse and clover, each kind in its season. I do not know if they garner the poppy's black dust. Jenkins says the pollens are mixed in the cells, which makes one wonder why the harvesters have to keep them apart. I wonder what the proportions are? Our bees are blessed, for they live in a paradise of flowers. I wish we could isolate the hives so as to get pure magnolia honey, mignonette, violet, azalea.

Once, in the south of France, I met a small dray drawn by a donkey, on which hives of differing colours were built up. The old man who walked beside the donkey told me that he goes to the orange groves first, then changes the sections and moves cart and bees on to white clover, or heather, according to season. He travels by night, so that he does not lose any of his bees. In the daytime he and the donkey sleep while the bees work. A crop-eared *chien de garde* keeps watch. One of his friends, he told me, has a hundred hives on a canal boat, but "for me the road", he said, and I agreed with him.

> Give me the wisdom of the bee,
> And her unwearied industry,
> That from the wild gourds of these days
> I may extract health, and Thy praise,
> Who can'st turn darkness into light,
> And in my weakness show Thy might.
> *Henry Vaughan, "The Bee"*

ALGY WAS a good judge of character. When Arthur Sandford first came to stay with us at Castle Freke, he knew that we had found a friend.

"He is so strong", Algy said, "that he makes me feel stronger directly he comes into the room. He doesn't treat me as if I were a sick man." Algy had a horror of being pitied. When we left Castle Freke on our last sad journey it was "Sandy" (as Algy called him) who took him to the boat in his brougham and carried him to the cabin. Algy, so tall but so thin, was like a child in those strong arms. The last time that he was out of doors – a week later, two days before he died, he lay through a long bright morning in his chair on the hillside – we were at West Malvern, looking at the blue distant hills of Wales.

"I wish Sandy was here," he said after a long silence, "I wish he was here to look after you. He is such a Big Brother."

That is what he has been to me, a big brother, an understanding friend, a tower of strength. Endless little things he has thought of to help me. Things for Jacky to do. "Isn't he old enough to have a pony? ... Wouldn't you ride with him? Riding is so good for one ... The hospitals are grateful for flowers ... would you care to send some, or bring them? The sick children? ... Do you ever come across patients for the Eye, Ear and Throat Hospital? Send them up or bring them. Wouldn't it be rather fun to bring a detachment of them to Cork one day? Lunatics? No! Are there any? How mad are they? Would you like to talk to Dr Woods about them at the Asylum?" One little suggestion after another to fill my desolate days.

JOHN HENNESSY is very poor. He has no home and no one to take care of him. He has inflamed eyes, and thinks my "eye-water" beats Dr Sandford's in Cork. Some say he is soft-like, which means a little less than daft.

He calls often for the price of a night's lodging. I realize it would be cheaper to find him a home.

I have remembered that there is a tiny, two-roomed cabin in the glen, which stands empty. Trees shadow it, a stream runs between its door and the road. The sun touches it in the morning. No one has lived there since it was "the sprigging school" fifty years ago.

One day I ask him, "Would you like a home of your own, John?"

"I would so, me lady, if you plazc."

"The cottage in the glen?"

"'Twould be grand, entoirely ... but ... 'tis a bit far."

"Far! It isn't two minutes from the village."

"Could I have the impty house there? 'Tis all the pities t'have it goin' to washte."

"Do you mean the Parish Room? No, John."

"That other one ... how would I pay the rint?"

"The rent would be a shilling a year."

"Glory to Goodness! A grand little house like that for a shillin' a year."

"Yes. A house and a bed, a table and a chair, a kettle ..."

"Faix, 'tis too much! Will I get it soon?"

"In a week."

Costello the carpenter has gone in to mend and glaze and whitewash. He is very silent and seems to know something that I don't. Duthie the steward is also silent. Old Jerry Spillane takes his "tar'ble foine harse under the cart" to fetch furniture and some coal. Jacky and I go to see the result.

A pillow, mattress and two grey blankets are on the bed. "I should like to live here myself," Jacky says, as we put the kettle on the hook and lay the table with a loaf and a pot of jam. John Hennessy is due to arrive at 4 o'clock.

Jacky: "He will walk in and look round and say, 'So this is my home! Angels have made my bed and laid my tea!' Will he say that, Mum?"

"Yes! He will have tears in his red eyes! He will say, 'John Hennessy, you're the lucky man to have such a grand little house.' "

It grows dark. At five we make up the fire and come away, leaving the door on the latch.

John Hennessy never took possession. His feelings were hurt! He never would have believed that the Ladyship would try to make him live in that *whisht* spot. What had she agin poor ould John that she should thry to force him to live where *They* come o' nights to dance and do their mischiefs!

So that was the reason the house had been empty year after year. It stands on fairy ground.

Costello knew, Duthie knew, everyone knew but me. They "made a hare of me".

A week later John Hennessy called for a bottle of "Lady Carberyship's eye-water" – and the price of a night's lodging.

"The hare" returned good for evil. But Carmody told the poor wretch what he thought of him.

OUR WOODS are called woods by courtesy; they are not much more than belts of trees. Yet they have character and beauty and each one its own spirit. Spirit isn't the right word ... it is that which is diffused through it and which makes itself known ... it is the wood but not the material wood. It is secret, shy and friendly to children and to sensitive spirits. Others it makes to be afraid.

There are places which people will not pass at night, where, they say, the wood holds and harbours ghosts. There is the White Lady who crosses the road to the garden and vanishes among the trees. She comes out of the ruined cottage which a century ago was the Priest's house. It stood then on the road from Ross to Milltown which John Lord Car-bery, called Lard Jan by the neighbours, diverted fifty years ago, and which came out where the Rectory garden is now. There was a gate across the road to save people from going headlong into the bog.

Just there, also, Lord John and his brother the Ould Captain, dead many a year, are said to ride on the ghosts of their favourite horses. Old Duggan can remember how, when he was a boy, they waited for him to open the gate for them. There was a moon that night, shining on their faces, and they smiled at him as they rode through. " 'That's little Duggan', Lord John said to the Ould Captain, an' the Ould Captain tuk a long look as he went by."

And through the wood below Croachna, a horseman rides. He comes from the back of the old castle, crosses where the causeway ran across what was then Lough Rahavarrig and follows the old buried road through the trees and over the hill. At the closed-up gateway he stops, for it was there he was murdered. But strange to say, the day he was murdered he was coming the reverse way to that travelled by the ghost, from the West. The gate had been tied, and cursing, he got off his horse. While he was fumbling with the string, a servant who had a grievance against his master sprang up from the shelter of the wall and killed him. The man had lain there hidden while his sister, who lived on the rock now called America, kept a look-out. When the master neared the gate she gave the signal. "Hoorig, hoorig," she cried, as tho' she was calling the pigs to their food.

I AM MELANCHOLY because I have to go to Castle Bernard [home of Lord and Lady Bandon] for a Saturday to Monday visit. To go away from home is grief to my spirit. I don't like going because I get so tired, and I dread practical jokes and what Beddoes rudely calls "idiot merriment", and William Watson, more politely, "barren levity of mind".

A party is happening. Tennis. Croquet. One hears fragments of talk. "Did you? Didn't you? Would you? Wouldn't you? Well, now! He said. She said." ... Doty Bandon is charming to her neighbours. The lawn is green and the trees splendid. Water-lilies shine on the pond, and gay ducks.

Mr Hurley is playing Liszt. No one listens, although he is making the piano talk. Lady M and Lady X, "bright and aged snakes", are dissecting reputations. People talk loudly, or whisper, which is worse.

Someone shuts the windows. People are hemming me in ... and stifling me ...

Dear God! Why am I not listening to the lapping of the tide on Ounahincha?

Dinner. My frock is lovely. Taylor has done my hair creditably. I am wearing my pearls. I miss Algy's approbation. I long to hear him sing as he used:

> Of all the gals that are so smart
> There's none like pretty Sally,
> She is the darlin' of my heart ...

The flowers are charming and the wonderful old Worcester plates a delight. Charles de Courcy, our footman, looks after me. I try hard to listen and to think of things to say. Nothing comes. I sit like a waxwork until my left-hand neighbour begins to talk. Then my brain thaws and my tongue uncurls. I can talk with the Canon [Besley] until tomorrow morning: books, poetry, folklore ... His "partner" won't have it! She seizes him. She is like a bat, dark and velvety, with sharp little white teeth. She is making the worst of him. Up in his room he has a notebook of amusing stories, which he scans when he is dressing for dinner. Lucas, a former butler of ours who also used to valet him, has seen it. No doubt Lucas drew on it for the edification of "the room" [term for upper servants' hall]. B. [Lord Bandon] winds the Canon up and the stories begin. I forget to listen and grow absent-minded. Nothing is real. People, voices, laughter – a noisy dream. I pinch myself; my heart is beating fast; in another moment I shall faint. It is the effect of people on me; some emanation, perhaps, which is hypnotic – if not poisonous. B. looks at Doty and coughs loudly until she attends and makes a move. The cooler air in the hall brings me back to reality.

The Canon talks to Doty and me while the rest play games. She knits, with thick wooden needles, unhurriedly and after the English manner, halves of crossovers which will eventually be sewn together into Christmas presents for the poor.

I am so tired. I feel myself unravelling, strand by strand. The dogs sit round with goggling eyes, mutely imploring to be walked out and put to bed.

At last we trail upstairs, candlesticks in hand; the men stand at the foot of the stairs admiring each his fancy, while B. tries to hustle them into the smoking-room.

SUNDAY. A blessed sleep until Lizzie with her sleeves rolled up brings scalding hot water for my bath. It is Sunday, but a day of toil for me. Taylor, my Scottish maid, is very cross. She doesn't like sharing the huge oval room with other visiting maids. She hates their ways and their gossip. We grump and do not speak.

Anyhow, she's lucky because she needn't go to church, and I must. The Canon preaches. A great sermon. Why don't we all grow into goodness after hearing tell of it?

Doty is good. She has all the fruits of the Spirit. She is the only person I know who has real humility. She has the grace of God.

In the afternoon we go to the garden, a trailing procession. The Pooles come to tea. Darling old Major P. and I have a delightful flirtation. He is over eighty. He is charming.

The Canon comes to dinner. We talk about nursery rhymes. "Green Gravel" is an ancient funeral hymn, and "Nuts in May" a relic of marriage by capture. "Ride-a-cock-horse", what was that? "Rot", B. said. But it was, as I explained to him, that cock horse is a usual name for the spare horse which was kept in readiness at the foot of steep Stanmore Hill to help the team of the incoming Birmingham mail-coach into Banbury.

MONDAY. The cobs and James McCarthy arrived at 10 a.m. They had to rest before doing the return journey, so I had a quiet and delightful morning with Doty, strolling about in the park and sitting on the lawn.

I drove the darling cobs home; they were very skittish. The osmunda and meadowsweet in the ditches were lovely; some late ragged robin with cotton grass in the boggy places. In the glen a heron was standing in the stream and rose with a great flapping of his wide wings and a *co-o-k*, which gave Puca an excuse to stand on his hind legs. Good little Pegasus dragged him on, before James could quite climb down from behind. He had one foot on the ground and one on the step and came hopping behind.

The children were at the lodge to drive back with me. "You've been away longer than you said," Jacky reproved me. "We expected you back to luncheon and there were lobster cucklets and poor Carmody was waiting at the door for hours and hours!" Baby only pressed lovingly against me. "Has I gwown?" (grown) he asked and added, "been a good baby".

I AM THANKFUL to be home again. Staying away anywhere is a misery to me and the normal country house life of sport and games and nothing much else is as foreign to me as fresh air to a fish. Yet I was brought up in a country house with Papa shooting, playing cricket, riding, and Mother riding, having school feasts and garden parties.

I think I was spoilt, or I should say emancipated from the country house atmosphere by being so much with the Curries; Cousin Cassie, the hermit, liking a few people very much, but not wanting to be with them over much, or for long together, liking someone to talk to at meals, and to be alone between whiles to read and write and think. Wrapt up in her family, and liking to have her "holy men".

Cousin Bertram, alert and full of life, spending his strenuous days in the city, coming home to the beloved family, to the peace of Coombe, to his books. Sometimes with one and another of his men friends, sometimes on Sundays people to luncheon or dinner, a few, all intelligent. Now and then a "banquet" for Mr Gladstone, or a party at Minley. Always such good talk, the G.O.M. Lord Granville, Lord Acton, Sir Anthony Godley, the Père Peter (archbishop of Bombay), Père Norris.

One never heard the word cricket, golf, tennis or bridge, very little if anything of plays or actors, or of new novels unless perhaps John Inglesant or Robert Elsmere, never noise or raised voices or chaffing or "jokes" or teasing or vexation. No drivel of any sort of kind. No talk about dogs.

A WONDERFUL NIGHT! I am happy to be at home and to smell the sweet weedy tang of the sea as I kneel at my open window. In the field the horses are lying down; the donkey is sleeping, his great head on the ground and his legs stretched out. A white owl flies noiselessly across the terrace. I hear – or do I dream it? – the faint singing of some small bird, possibly a sedge-warbler beside the stream. The Irish call it "night-singer" because it sings after darkness has fallen. It is good to be at home.

> I looked abroad upon the wide old world,
> And in the sky and sea, through the same clouds,
> The same stars saw I glistening, and naught else.
> And as my soul sighed unto the world's soul,
> Far in the north a wind blackened the water.

I am glad to see the same stars. But the wind which blackens these western waters is cold and sends me to my bed. Jacky, half waking in his little bed, puts out his hand to find mine and so we fall asleep.

FROM OUTSIDE, people with hooks and lines catch me to do things. Tomorrow I have to open a bazaar at Skibbereen; on Thursday there are two committees in Cork. Doty is an active caster-of-nets. She entangles me in hateful committees where women talk and talk, mostly to one another, and waste time over matters which could be settled in ten minutes by two sensible people. Or by one! I observe that women behave better when there are men on the committee, but even then there is no briskness.

Apart from these entanglements there are others. I am trapped by Sense of Duty, that dull dogger of steps; I am held by the Call of Misery from far and near.

A LONG AFTERNOON, visiting "the neighbours".

Mrs Duggan wants to buy a "Y'ung doonkey, a child of Egypt". Egypt is our great black Egyptian Jack donkey. She wants a "boy doonkey", one of the three Egyptian stallions I bought to improve the local stock. She has done with her own "little female ass" (from which she had hoped for a "half-Egyptian" foal), "She do be for ever gettin' into throuble wid the small little Irish Jacks! These two years she have poor Dooggan frustrated ... an' she lookin' at us so innicent wid her face!"

Mrs Patrick Donovan's girl is no better. "'Tis the quare thing she'd be distant in her mind! The quare notions she do be takin'! An' worse when the wind blows ... the dark wind at night ... an' the shadows ..." The poor woman cried.

The child is going to Cork next week ... "When she'll have the clothes an' the boots from Clonakilty, thanks be to your ladyship an' God." It is more polite in speaking to me to put me first and God second.

From Mrs Donovan I drove round by Galley Head. The day was soft and damp. The sea was heaving and sobbing in the small coves and moaning dismally in the seal's cave where the blow-hole is. On the tiny beach the fishermen were dragging their boats out of the tide's reach. One of them came to speak to me. He pointed to the stormy sunset and showed me "the shadow of rain coming up on the wind", and advised me to get home as quick as I could. "Not but what your ladyship is hardy, but there's the harse, and James McCarthy wearin' his fine coat."

I HAD GONE OUT chiefly to see old Dinny whose wife died early this morning. Mrs Leary, the fisherwoman, brought the news. Mary Dinny was a plain woman, with squinny eyes and snaggle teeth; coming from the county Kildare, she was looked upon as a foreigner. Dinny and Mary loved one another very much but they were lonely for the four children who went long ago to America. At first they wrote often and from time to time sent home little presents of money. They "were getting on fine; they were going to be married; they had babies; they were lucky to be in good places". Then, times were not so good. One by one they left off writing.

Then, perhaps, a neighbour's son or daughter "out there" might send a word of news. After that, silence. I tried through one way or another to trace them, but in vain. "If we c'd know how it is wid them ... if they be livin' or dead, or what way it is at all!"

The door was open, letting in a long beam of the westering sun. A turf-fire smouldered on the hearth under the swinging kettle, a loaf and a twist of sugar were on the table beside a battered tea-pot. The room was empty but for a couple of hens.

From the inner room came the sound of Dinny's voice. It was dim in there, for the pane of glass fixed into the wall, which did duty for a window, let in little light. The air was stale and acrid. Dinny sat on a box wedged between bed and wall; his grey head was on the pillow. Someone had shut his wife's squinny eyes and laid pennies on the lids; her arms, her toil-worn hands were lying stiffly on either side of her; her lips were drawn up showing the wolf-like fangs.

"Me darlin', me darlin'," the old man was murmuring, "me lovely one ... whatever'll happen me widout ye?" He looked up and saw me. "Here's the ladyship come to see us," he said to the white thing on the bed, getting up. Poor Dinny! Poor, dazed Dinny! He squeezed along the wall and stood beside me at the foot of the bed; we looked at her together. "An' she to be tuk from me that have the great need of her ... 'tis the quare thing," he said. "An' what will I do ... och! what will I do alone in the house wid meself?"

One of his neighbours has come in to make his tea; there is minced beef in a jar which James McCarthy brought from the well of the car, to be spread on his bread, or to be heated in the embers. Katie will comfort Dinny with her homely words better than I can. He comes out to the car with me, a dirty, dishevelled old man, with the fine manners of his race.

"Ye'll forgive me bein' a bit moidhered," he said as he put the rug over my knees. Then he looked up at the angry sky. "Get ye home, James McCarthy," he said, "for there's a great rain comin' on the dark wind of night ... a dark wind an' a great rain, an' gloom over all the world."

BETTER WEATHER NOW. The air is full of cuckoo-call. I heard it at dawn, and later above the *bourdon* of the mowing-machine on the terrace. Cuckoos flew about my head when I was riding over the cliffs this morning. Near the West Lodge I saw one sitting on the wall, being heckled by a mob of small birds. He pecked crossly this way and that but was forced by their buffeting wings to move on.

In number there are nine cock-cuckoos to one hen. She, poor thing, is born to be flighty. She has none of the joys of home-making birds. Although she is spared the labour and anxiety of bringing up a family, the worry of having nine possible mates must be appalling.

"The cuckoo calls aloud his wandering love," writes Ambrose Philips. In Scotland cuckoos are called gowks. The Scot, stingy with words, says, "Hear the gowks yell!"

JACKY AND I walk by the lake road and we sit for a time beside Kilkerran. Larks are singing in the heights. On the water are gulls and cormorants and a fleet of tame ducks from the Battery.

Jacky asks, how it is that no big birds sing?

I say that I don't know.

"If I had been God," Jacky says, "I should have given them all voices. A gull would spatter out quite as good a song as a lark if God had given it the right sort of throat."

If cormorants could sing, what a song! I can imagine them, bass and throaty, but fine, like bassoons.

MY LOOKING-GLASS is oval, large for so old a glass, in an inlaid frame. It is an upright, fair glass which neither flatters nor slanders.

It is a precious thing to me because it has reflected Algy's face and my own beside his, young and happy.

KITTY is like a sister to me. She is my beautiful brown mare, bought from A.S. [Arthur Sandford], who pretended that an imaginary owner "did not particularly want to sell but his stables are full". "She is charming to ride," he wrote. "Did you see the sunset last night?" I like that inconsequence.

So one golden evening when Jacky and I were awaiting her arrival, she emerged from the wood, a lovely gentle creature, staring about her, her ears moving to catch the whinnying of the horse-folk in the stables as Nobbs and his followers ran out to welcome her.

"Doctor Sandford", said Nobbs standing back to admire her, "is a reel good judge of a hoss!" He ran his expert hands up and down her slender legs.

"She's wearin' the docther's knee caps," observed James McCarthy.

Jacky said, "Kitty is very large! She must be a he-horse I think."

She is a godsend to me. Every morning at 7.45 she takes me for a ride. We go alone, usually over the cliffs, sometimes by lanes and bo'reens so narrow that there is scarcely room to pass the cows and donkeys that are breakfasting from the high banks on either side.

At first there was great surprise that I should be out so early when I might be in my bed, and much questioning of my motive. "Is it to see are the men at their work in good time? Or mebbe 'tis to regulate Mr D. (the steward), or to look are the lodge gates open before her? Or to encourage Mr Nobbs in his English ways, bringin' the boys from their beds be 6 o'clock, robbin' them and the harses of their rest, and the moon yet in the sky!"

But after a time they got used to seeing Kitty and her rider on the cliffs, etched in black on the crimson of a winter sunrise, or cantering through a shower that is mostly rainbow, or making an early sick call at the door of a cabin.

WHAT IS THE USE of being a member of the Church of England if it does not save one from being scolded by a priest of the Church of Rome? Today Father O'Hea called to see me. He hardly ever comes here because he is a Nationalist and has no use for landlords. As I came down the stairs I heard him striding about. He had come to reprove me for lending £8 to one of his parishioners, Michael Brien.

Brien is a small farmer who lives near the Red Strand with his only child, a hump-backed boy. His wife has been dead a long time, he said; he and the boy are alone together and no woman to mind them. He looked apologetically at his ragged sleeve when he came recently to tell me his troubles. The Bank had been pressing him for repayment of a loan. He was anxious in his mind, having no means of raising the money. Would I help him by lending him £8? I said I would. I was very cautious and made out the cheque to the Bank.

Brien is much more than a farmer, he is "a sort of scholar", believed to speak, read and write the Irish, knowing a great deal of Irish history and local folklore. Very diffidently he suggested a way to pay off the loan, or part of it, by becoming my tutor and teaching me all this and more. My curiosity was roused.

If Queen Victoria can learn Hindustani I can learn Irish. I have already been taught to say "In the name of the Father and of the Son" in Irish, and the right way to make the sign of the Cross by a sick woman whom I visit, and I have learned how to bless haymakers, roadmenders, in fact anyone at work: "Bail o'dhia ag an obair," God bless the work. To pass by without saying this would bring bad luck. Sweet sounding words, all of them.

I agreed to Brien's suggestion, and now twice a week he comes in his funeral coat, his face washed, his beard trimmed, to instruct me. We work in the saloon. The letters are pleasant to write, characteristic, with a ruggedness which makes them only a little less beautiful than Greek lettering, which I learned at an early age. My timetable is, copy-writing ten minutes, words and pronunciation twenty minutes, folklore fifteen minutes, history of Ireland – as long as Brien chooses, or until Carmody intervenes to save me from collapse.

"Your ladyship is wanted," he says solemnly. Brien retires and I hope Carmody gives him a glass of port. Beer and stout are strictly prohibited. Before our time Castle Freke had a bad reputation for the "lashans of drink" obtainable there. Algy stopped it once and for all.

And now here comes Father O'Hea to rate me. I listen dutifully, knowing that in principle he is right, and praying that he has not heard of two or three other loans in the neighbourhood for the purchase of a little cow, or the payment of a rent to save a family from eviction.

I tell him also that the transaction cannot be looked upon as a common loan; it is prepayment for lessons in Irish history and language.

He is surprised, and I fear rather sceptical of my success in mastering a language in which I believe he is not too proficient himself. We part good friends, at least I hope so.

THIS MORNING, as Kitty and I were coming home by the myrtle grove, old Paddy stopped his raking to speak to me.

He was mysterious and clearly afraid to say all that was in his mind, but I gathered that he wished me to go to his neighbour, Mrs Katty Donovan, and find out what is the matter with her baby.

"Is it ill?" I asked.

"No, then, 'tis not ill, 'tis a small little baby ... there's throuble," he said, "an' t'will be worse tomorrow than it is today."

Evidently there was no time to lose, so after breakfast I set off on my errand. When I went in to the poor cabin the baby was crying weakly in its bed made from a wooden box. Katty crouched by the fire.

"Are you ill, Katty?" I asked her.

"No, then ..."

"Is Baby ill? Tell me your trouble, Katty."

"She's small .... she have a great hunger all the time ..."

Katty looked in my face with heavy eyes to see if I understood. "The night she was born there was a great storm ... himself would not go out to untie the horse an' the donkey ... he would have the door kept shut – the soft little man – while the baby was comin', an' meself had me hair plaited, forgettin' in me trouble to let it loose, God help me."

Opening doors and windows, untying cattle that are fastened, loosening plaits of hair, are birth customs. Many people believe that anything shut or tied up will prevent the spirit from entering the body of the newly born. Fairies (*They*, for no one will call them fairies) seize the chance and steal the spirit, leaving a changeling in its place. To get rid of the changeling the child must be made to laugh or sneeze, otherwise it is held over the fire until, screaming, the fairy goes out.

"So, outside was the soul av the baby tryin' and tryin' to get in," Katty continued, "the soul av the baby ... shut out in the night an' the storm."

"No, Katty, no ..."

"'Tis the truth ... 'tis then that They took the soul av me baby an' left me ... that in its place. At first I saw no difference, but now ... herself so small ... wid the great hunger an' screamin' an' cryin' ... an' never a sneeze, and never a smile on her face ... The neighbours do be comin' an' thrustin' in their faces at the door to ask, 'have she sneezed yet? Have she smiled?'"

"How can she smile, the poor little baby, when she is so hungry? When did you feed her last?"

"'Twas yesterday, then," Katty murmured.

"*Yesterday*! But why, Katty? Can't you nurse her any longer?"

"Nurse her, is it? I'd be glad to ease the pain in me breast ..." She began to cry. "I wanted to give her the chanst of dyin' before ... before ..."

"Yes, before?"

"Before they come ... tonight ... to try her ... over the fire ... to try is she ... is she ... one of *Them*."

"Who are coming?"

"The neighbours. Himself will not be iddin ... 'tis the night he stays late at the shop. I'm to have the ... the fire ready by seven o'clock ..."

The baby's weak wailing broke a dreadful silence.

"Katty," I said to her at last, "listen to me. This baby is your own; God doesn't let *Them* steal little children. It is all a mistake. You must believe that what I am saying to you is the truth. Before it is too late you must save your baby's life. If you let her die you will be a murderer. Come, sit up on the chair."

Katty got up from the hearth and stood watching me – then she subsided on a chair. I took the sodden baby out of its box and held it, talking to it, and taking no notice of its mother, until I saw her fumbling at her dress. A few moments later there was no sound in the cabin but the tiny noise made by a baby's lips. Katty's eyes were shut; slow tears coursed down her cheeks. All too soon I had to take the starved baby away from her, or it might have died from over-feeding. Together we undressed it, washed it and put it into a cleaner bed; and while I minded it, Katty went to tell the neighbours that there would be no testing of the baby, whom she knew to be her own.

As she came back into the cabin there was a tiny sneeze from the bed.

As a matter of precaution, I rode on to tell Father O'Brien what had happened. He didn't laugh as I half-feared he might.

"I will be round there tonight," he said, "to make sure there are no haythen doings in this parish. God forgive me that I have not cured them of their superstitions after forty years among them."

I made him promise to say nothing and not to scold poor Katty.

A PERFECT MAY DAY. The woods are in their utmost beauty. I had to come indoors, to leave the bluebells in their amazing loveliness, afraid, because my spirit seemed to come too close to a great mystery, too near to fathoming a secret withheld by God's mercy. Thwarted, sorrowful and very humble, one retreats and busies oneself with a trivial task, striving to re-enter the routine of living, while the Guardian of the Temple receives the nearly-escaped Spirit, with gentle pity folding the still-fluttering wings. Such a curious dream I had last night. I saw the dead body of R.B. lying on a pavement in London with a policeman standing by. The houses in the street were Georgian, I saw the fanlights over the doors. No one was about. The body lay on its chest, the face resting on one cheek on the pavement, the hands out on either side. It lay in a scatter of gay, autumn leaves. I said to the policeman:

"Where do these red leaves come from? I thought it was Spring!"

"It's Spring, right enough," the policeman answered, "those aren't leaves, they're sins. Fallen off 'im," he added, stirring them with his square-toed boot.

Insignificant, they seemed, those dead symbols of hatred and lying and lust. One was glad they had fallen off, that he had done with evil and had passed on with the good that was in him.

MY SPIRIT has lately been kept too much on the chain. This morning I escaped from E. into the wood.

"Ah, dearie," she said when I came in, blinking her white eyelashes, "You have been in the wood to pick bluebells, I suppose."

I wonder why she thought that; my hands were empty, and one doesn't gather bluebells because it is bad for their bulbs. She would never be able to understand that one goes to gather beauty and peace. Not only that. One's chained spirit must be loosed. Its body is left on a fallen tree, an empty husk to be recharged with energy from the earth, while the exulting spirit is dispersed in the great sea of bluebells, reaching away and away under the greening beech trees, a sea of blueness and fragrance and indescribable loveliness.

IN THE AFTERNOON we drove to have tea with a distant neighbour, Willie Townshend. His wife was the haughty sister of Lord Curzon, and their nickname is Prunes and Prisms. While E. and our hostess talked about the Y.W.C.A., the China Inland Mission, and all that, our host took me to the fields to see his mares. It was late when we got home. E. was tired and went to her room for what she calls "a lie-down". She asked to have dinner put off and for us not to dress.

I went to the garden, running all the way there as there was no one about to think me outrageous. The flowers were falling asleep. In the twilight their faces were dun. They were like changelings. I picked rosemary for my room. Then I panted back up the steep road, changed into a high-necked frock to please my guest and spent a wretched evening alone with her.

OUNAHINCHA. Of all the mystic places and dear to my heart, Ounahincha is most dear, and the rocky strand where Ounahincha water meets the sea. I can sit there, hour upon hour, brooding over the stream, and while I am conscious, vividly conscious, of its voice against the sea's voice, of its changing and varied colour, of every swish and ripple on its surface and of the flat, many-hued stones in its bed, I can think of things which have nothing to do with itself, yet are hallowed and made beautiful by being associated with it.

Old is the stream, young are its waters. Their life is measured by one long summer day with its night. From a fern-trimmed rock they well; they force a way through a tangle of briar and foxglove into a heathery lane in whose length they gather small rills from the meadows, keeping kind company the while with labourers and wayfaring men. Under the Hill of the Cromlech the brown bog receives them. Faster they flow with the falling ground and fast over shingle and sand, until they are received, those sweet young waters, into the Great Bitterness.

I AM a stern taskmaster to myself. I keep my own nose to the grindstone and only when the morning's work is done, do I allow myself to go out.

The work includes keeping accounts; answering letters; attending, in their turn, to my branch of the Needlework Guild, and the Industrial Association; providing work for the weavers and knitters, besides seeing about household matters, and doing things for poor people. These things have to be done before I can go out, or play the organ, or settle down to read. The mornings are too short for all I must do, and often I am miserably tired.

Now that Jacky does lessons I have more time. His first governess was a failure, neither he nor I could endure her; now he has a delightful old tutor, who comes daily from Clonakilty. He is a cousin of the great Miss Hungerford "of the Island", six foot two, and thin and active. Jacky likes to go out with him, "because he knows about things".

On wet days Baby plays on the floor while I write. Today I met Mrs Duggan in the shrubbery. She likes to walk there because she was born in the Keeper's house close by. It makes her feel young again.

"When I am dead," she said to me, "an' when I am let see Almighty God, I'll ask Him, will Your Honour let me go back to the shrubbery at Castle Freke, for that'd be more to me mind than Heaven, be it iver so fine and grand! Ye'd not mind me wanderin' about, me lady, nor be afeard to meet me?"

"Not I."

We arranged to meet, in some future time, and to speak if we can, at Miss Kitty's garden. Miss Kitty, a child of the Ould Captain, has been dead these fifty years, yet a mossy patch in the shrubbery is still known as "Miss Kitty's garden".

I am to try hard to see her and she will try hard to speak to me, "An' sure Almighty God wouldn't be harsh! He would be glad to let ould friends meet once again ... an' seein' He lets Lord Jan and th'ould Captain ride their same ould harses about the place. Did not Dooggan himself as a boy open the gate to them?"

We both looked over our shoulders, thinking we heard the ghostly horses. "Faix," she said, laughing, "'tis the young colts in the kennel-field playin' thricks on us." Then her face changed and she said, "It's lonesome for ye, me lady, walkin' ayst and west, and narth and south, the way ye do, alone day by day ..."

ON A LOVELY peacock day such as this I want to be in splendid company. In the twinkling of an eye the four Archangels appear, looking like Persian firebirds, whose Persian names I don't know, so I call them by their ceremonious Arabic names: Israfil, Azrail, Mikail, Jibrail – or, for short, Isra, Azra, Mick and Jib.

Come ye, Israfil, Azrail, Mikail and Jibrail, in your flaming garments; come my plain, my everyday Angel in your homespun coat, dear guardian with your slanting, gypsy eyes and your crooked smile; come Ip, my darling, and let us make a procession round the garden to the trumpeting of Amaryllis, the ringing of lily bells, the clash of the bird orchestra,

> threstill with her warblynge
> mavis with her whistell

and the happy shouting of the children.

What a charming company we are! Jacky, dragging a scarlet engine, Baby in his perambulator, Nanny and two little Jenkins boys and Roy the fox-terrier, holding our own among the Lordly Ones.

WHERE IN OR ABOUT ME are my sense-stores? Where do I keep scent-impressions? Magnolia, violet, lavender, hayfield, beanfield, white clover? And a hundred others; the scent of May morning, of wet woods, of minty river, seaweed, peat-smoke, burning weeds, cedar, incense, snow?

They are stored in my treasury; distinct and certain scent-impressions, not the actual smell, but the idea of it.

Also, I have a colour treasury. I seem to be constantly going to it. It is an exquisite possession. Here sound and idea are associated, as in the scent-treasury. Bird-song, cuckoo-cry, the hunting-hoot of owls, the sound of wind and wave and the chatter of small streams, the high cry of grasshoppers on a summer alp, music, the voices of those whom I love.

I compare one shade with another, I mingle my colours and rejoice in their beauty and variety. But there is one colour missing which I have seen in dreams and for which there is no name, nor can I remember it at all distinctly in waking hours.

These storehouses seem to be set apart from the great treasury of memory whose door is less well guarded, so that recollections slip out for a time, or for ever. Those that remain inside are apt to fade, their outlines become blurred. Strangely, too, they change their character. That which was once pain loses its sting and what once seemed a curse becomes a blessing.

The door of the treasury of memory stands ajar; through it steal old hatreds, jealousies and contempts. The last of the dark inhabitants to creep away are superstitions; a few of these, once fearsome, now amusing, go no further than the lumber room of memory, where they lie beside outworn yet dear beliefs.

There are memories one would gladly lose yet cannot oust: of hurts one has dealt, of impatient and unkind words, of charity refused, a child disappointed. Still more tenacious are the recollection of *faux pas*, and of humiliations experienced in childhood. These seem burnt in to one.

There is a great loneliness about the place of memory. How dear to all of us are the few who have shared the same happy experiences and have counterpart recollections! What a link between parents and children, brothers and sisters, friends, lovers!

The memory of happenings belong to us individually but surely also to life. It may be that life carries them on to a greater treasury where the impressions of all action and all thought are stored, in the same way that in me is laid up the remembrance of the pale gold of my babies' curls; the sound of a beloved voice; the poignant scent of *immortelles*.

ONE OF THOSE states of mind and body which are hard to account for. Going down alone to the sea with a tired body and a heavy heart, stepping carefully down the cliffside from rock to rock, from ledge to ledge until the fine grey gravel is under one's feet. Standing with eyes on the incoming tide, and ears filled with the voice of many waters, all sense of I-me is numbed; I am merged in the sea, rising and falling with green, translucent waves, breaking on the farther rocks, on the nearer rocks, flattening, foaming and spreading; sweeping seawards again with a roar of pebbles, reaching up, rising up in might, curling over, falling – gloriously obeying and fulfilling.

Spray – stinging, cold, salt, is tossed to the empty body which stands motionless at the water's edge until the ninth wave drives it back. It turns away, the absent mind comes back – and is astonished to see land.

BRIEN, my teacher of Irish, is a born story-teller. After my laborious and usually unsuccessful efforts to twist my tongue to the sounds of this wild language, and after he has examined my written exercises – "Haven't ye the grand success with *the letters*?" – he rewards my industry by telling me the True History of Eire and How Eire Came To Be Populated.

"Will I begin at the beginning?" he asked at the first lesson, "or will I begin somewheres in the middle times?"

"At the beginning. I don't want to miss anything. And I hope you won't teach me in the words of a book but out of your head, in real, everyday words – if you don't mind."

"There's not another Sassanach in the country will know the half of what ye will know be the time I have done instructin' ye."

"And you won't mind my taking notes?"

He seemed gratified. "I willn't mind at all."

"There isn't much I can tell ye about the Creation of the World that ye haven't learnt from the Bible; all the same there's persons now livin' who do be sayin' that Eire was larger be far in them early days, stretchin' away and away, swallyin' England entirely, till she come to join on with France and Germany. Westward, too, she stretched, but not far. I've heard tell that what stopped her joinin' on to America was respect for Moy Mell, not being wishful to intrude on that Land of the Blessed Dead – God rest their souls – Moy Mell lyin', as ye know, not so very far beyond Toe Head and our own familiar sea.

"Sure Ireland was a fine land in them first days, the way Almighty God intended her to be, a grand, great continent in herself. How she came to shrink the way she have was not by His intention. And for domestic animals she had the great hairy elephant, and elks and hyenas, and dragons blowin' flames out of their throats, and snakes in plenty and many great and strange worrums."

"I will now pass on to the Flood. 'Tis a quare thing that hardly any one knows that Noah was not the only man to build an ark!"

He paused. I felt and expressed great surprise.

"There was a man called Bith," Brien spoke in a mysterious whisper, "and Bith was a friend of the ould prophet Noah. Bith lived in a wood near to the seashore with his wife, Barran, and his two brothers, Ladhra and Fiontain, whose wives were called Balbha and Caesar. One day Noah came to see his friend Bith. He was wantin' gopher trees out of Bith's wood.

" 'What will ye be wantin' with gopher wood?' asked Bith, who was a cautious sort of a man.

" 'If ye must know,' answers Noah, 'I've had orders to build a ship called an Ark. She's to be built of gopher wood and no other. Judgin' by the measurements, I'll be wantin' all the gopher wood I can lay me hands on, for me ark is to be built in three storeys, one above another and strong as may be to hould the weight of the quare company that's comin' aboard.'

" 'Company?' says Bith, 'what sort o' company?'

" 'There'll be camels,' answers Noah, 'and harses and doonkeys and cows and all manner of wild beasts, birds and insects, male and female, clean and unclean, for stockin' the world, and seven of every kind for provisions for the voyage. And of course me wife and me family will be there to help me with the management of me ark.'

" ''Tis strange words ye do be talkin',' says Bith, 'but no doubt ye've had y'orders, though it's the quare thing for an aged ould man like y'self to go sailin' away with sich a rigiment to command!'

" ''Tis true that I do be gettin' on in years,' says Noah, a bit put out, 'but I am not too ould to do the biddin' of me God!'

" 'Och! Him!' says Bith wid respect.

" 'Me God,' says Noah, speakin' very solemn and serious, 'warns me there is goin' to be a great flood over all the world; for forty days and nights the rain will be fallin', and all the people in the world will be drowned on account of their sins, barrin' me and me family. Every livin' creature will be drowned barrin' them that I'm takin' two by two and seven by seven into the ark.'

"'Och! musha!' cries Bith, 'if that doesn't bate all! 'Twould be grand in them days to be a fish! But look ye, Noah, you're growin' an ould man; 'twould come hard on ye to be fellin' trees and haulin' heavy timber an' mebbe the head turnin' on ye when ye'd be busy aloft on the scaffold. I'm thinkin' ye'd best sit aisy on the dyke and direct the buildin' while meself and me two brothers do be workin' with yer three sons. And', says Bith, seein' that Noah wasn't answerin' him, 'ye can have me gopher wood, every stick of it, and all I'll be askin' in return is a small little room in the ark where meself an' me brothers and our children can be saved with you an' y' family.'

"'Och! och! my grief!' says Noah, groanin', 'and you me ould friend and neighbour! But never a word did me God speak me to save you! That's the truth an' no lie! ... So there y'are!'

Bith thought a bit, being a cautious, far-seein' sort of a man. 'Well,' says he at last, 'ould friend and neighbour ye may be, but ye'll have to go some-wheres else for y' gopher wood. I'll be needin' me own gopher wood for the buildin' of me own ark!'

"'If that's y' last word, neighbour,' says Noah, 'I'll be hittin' the road, and wishin' ye good luck!' With that the good ould prophet went stridin' away, while Bith stood lookin' after him with pity in his heart for thinkin' of the hardship and the troubles lyin' in wait for him, when the rain would be fallin' and the sea lashin' and roarin', when the light of moon and stars would be quenched and mebbe the face of his God lost to him in the cloud and darkness.

"When Noah was gone out of sight, Bith made haste to tell Barran, his wife, all that had passed between them and of his plan to cut down the gopher trees so as to build an ark for themselves. Now Barran had a great likin' for her home in the wood and she did not wish her fine trees cut down for mebbe a rumour. So she said, 'I'm thinkin', Bith, we will first go ask our own Idol is it the truth that ould Noah do be tellin' ye.' So they set off together and before long they came to the Idol's house, and the priest who had care of the Idol brought them in and let them take a quick look at the Idol, and set out the bowl for their offerings, and told them to sit down on the floor. Then Bith told the Idol every word that Noah had said, and while Barran was layin' some little present in the Idol's bowl, Bith asked: 'Is it the truth that there will be a flood over all the world and will every person be drowned?'

" 'If Noah's God says there will be a flood,' answered the Idol in a snorin' little voice, 'I would expect that there will be a flood, and one that will drown them that is caught unprepared.'

" 'Thank ye, ma'am,' says Bith, 'and if I may make so bould, I take it ye'd advise me to set about buildin' some sort of a ship or an ark?'

" ''An ark,' mutters the Idol, who was comin' over drowsy, 'or some ... sort ... of a ship.'

"That was the end of the visit, for the priest who cared for the Idol let fall a curtain and came out for the bowl and to look was the present big enough, and to ask Bith would he take him and the Idol in his ark? Bith, bein' a cautious sort of a man, would not make any promises. On the way home he asked his wife did she think that snufflin' voice came from the Idol, or was the priest talkin' for her, and was the Idol nobbut a painted image with no life in her? Barran thought the Idol might be an image but she did not think the priest would impose on them. And when Bith asked her her reason for thinkin' so highly of the man, she said 'twas a feelin' she had, and hadn't he the fine pair of eyes and the grand commandin' way with him?

After a year or so Bith's ark was built and reared up on the beach ready for travellin' down the rollers to the sea. Bith was so satisfied with his ark that he was wishful to set off on the voyage and not be waitin' for the flood to set in. So he sent word around that he had employment for a crew of fifteen or twenty sea-farin' men. Now Bith's ark, not havin' to take in cattle and wild beasts, was not so high nor so square and clumsy-lookin' as the ark that Noah was labourin' on, and it was not so ould-fashioned and uncontrolled as directed on Noah's plans. In the middle of the roof of Bith's ark was a platform for the look-out man, and standin' up through the roof was a couple of chimneys and two masts with a number of sails of every shape and size for, as Bith said to Barran, who sewed them, 'sure, there's safety in numbers and between all the varyin' shapes there'll be some that the crew, bein' used to handlin' ships, will find convenient to the wind. And there's ropes and twine hangin' in readiness from the mast and from the crossway poles.'

"In the forefront of Bith's ark was carved a risin' sun with his rays, and at the rear of the ship was a great steerin' oar and a rudder below it. Inside was the rooms for the family and a great hall for the crew and a room full of flour and wine and oil and nuts and dried hake and dried peas.

"'Well now, well now indeed,' says Bith, lookin' round him with pride, 'I'm thinkin' we will be startin' the morrow's morn for the voyage.' All the same he felt onaisy for ne'er a one of the crew had arrived. So he instructed his brothers to call in at every drinkin' place where there'd likely be seafarin' men and to fetch twenty of them to the ship. 'Ye can tell them,' he said, 'about the flood that's comin', and ye can warn them of their sins, if so be they hang back at all.'

"You'd think that solemn warnin' about the flood, when they'd be drowned whether or no, would have made them come racin' and leppin' to the ship? They did nothin' of the sort! The men of that land were wine-bibbers and slothful, as the Bible says of them, and nothing would stir them into activity.

" 'There's others that are willin' to come,' says Fiontain and Ladhra together, returnin' to the ark and lookin' pleased and yet a bit sheep-faced. Before they could say another word, fifty beautiful venturesome ladies came runnin' to Bith, offerin' to do the work of men about the ship. Before Bith could get his breath they were swarmin' over the ark, each one carryin' a leather bag and over her arm a fine white sheepskin for beddin'. Bith turned for advice to Barran, who saw no reason for delay. She had a feelin', she said, that fifty women could do the work of twenty men if they tried.

"After the crew had gone to their hall and shaken out their robes and settled the sheepskins in their hammocks, and after the wives and children of Bith and his brothers had come on board, and as there was a favourable wind gettin' up, Bith gave the word to start, standin' on the platform, while Fiontain stood at the steerin' oar behind and Ladhra, holdin' fast by a rope attached to the mast, started the ship rollin' down the rollers to the sea, before he was hauled up by the fifty beautiful ladies, pullin' on the rope like one man.

"Bith's ark set off very fast but it wasn't more'n a few miles away when it ceased to go forward, and it turned round and round and round, owin' to some irregularity in the way Bith had the sails hung, or mebbe 'twas due to a whirlpool. And the crew lay cryin' in their hammocks. Durin' the night a breeze filled some of the sails of the ark and bore her onward and ever onward accordin' to the way of the wind. The crew, for want of skill in navigation, could not furl or lower the sails, nor was there one among them that could so much as tie a knot, and the wind being more strong than the steerin' oar, they let steerin' alone. In this way for seven years they were tossed and driven by the wind, till at last the ship ran high and dry on the shore of Eire and there's them that think mebbe 'twas between Kinsale and Galley Head, possibly Courtmacsherry or Clonakilty or even on the Red Strand near me own little farm.

"When I shut me eyes," Brien said, shutting them, "I can see that landin' of the first men and women to set foot in this land. I can see ould Bith with a beard on him as long as me arm, standin' on his platform givin' commands. I can see Fiontain at the bottom of the landin' plank, receivin' Barran and Balbha and Caesar, the wives, and I see Ladhra at the top of the plank, keepin' the crew back to follow in their turn, and them clamourin' to know what'll happen them now they'd come to land.

" 'First of all,' says Bith, 'we'll walk straight ahead till we come to a town or a shebeen', and little he knew that the land was empty from end to end but for the creatures set there by Almighty God.

"So they walked on till they came to the meetin' of two rivers and there Bith divided them into three parties to spy out the land: he and Barran chose seventeen of the beautiful venturesome ladies to be of their party; Fiontain and Caesar, his wife, chose another seventeen of them, and Ladhra took the remaining sixteen with Balbha his wife. They set off in different directions. 'Tis a great pity that not one of the ould histories tell of their adventures, leavin' us to conjecture for ourselves, but we know that before long Ladhra died and Balbha, his widow, sent eight of the ladies to Fiontain; herself and the remaining eight ladies joined on with Bith, so it looks like the three parties were within easy reach of one another. Before long poor ould Bith went west, the leader of them all, and a man of courage and skill even though he was a h'athen and consulted with Idols. This time there were the two widow-women and thirty-three beautiful venturesome ladies left defenceless at the mercy of wild beasts and likely to starve with no man to defend them and provide nourishment for them. The sooner they could join themselves with Fiontain the better, they agreed, so after buryin' Bith in a cave, which was the way they buried in the land they come from, they went off to find Fiontain. It wasn't long before, from a hill's top, they looked down upon the place where Fiontain was camped. Barran and Balbha, the widows, cried from afar that they were comin' to live with him for the rest of their days.

"Fiontain, seein' those thirty-five women approachin' at great speed down the hill, fled without a word.

"And while he was escapin', and Barran, Balbha and Caesar were chasin' after him with the fifty beautiful venturesome ladies, the Flood of Noah reached the land of Eire. Risin' ... and risin' ... and risin' ... it overwhelmed them all."

> Not as all other women are
> Is she that to my soul is dear,
> Her glorious fancies come from far
> Beneath the silver evening-star,
> And yet her heart is ever near.
>
> She doeth little kindnesses
> Which most leave undone, or despise,
> For naught that sets one heart at ease
> And giveth happiness or peace,
> Is low esteemed in her eyes.
>
> She hath no scorn of common things,
> And though she seem of other birth,
> Round us her heart entwines and clings,
> And patiently she folds her wings
> To tread the humble path of earth.

THESE WORDS of Lowell's describe my own mother exactly – the second and third verses particularly. She has come to stay with me. She has come in her goodness, her simplicity, her happiness, her reticence, her kindness. Her paths are paths of peace.

Everyone loves her. Jacky calls her Mother. When I said, "She is your grandmother," he scoffed. "She isn't. She is Mother, all-of-our Mother." He is right.

Her "glorious fancies" are there, but they are not from her own imagination. They "come from far", from the Bible, largely. She does not spin them from her own brain. She can see the Celestial City with its gates of pearl, the boys and girls playing in the streets, horses with gold bells about their necks, harpers playing and singing her favourite hymns.

She would see and hear all that she had heard and read about the City of God, Jerusalem the Golden, green pastures, the waters of comfort. She can see those she has loved and lost awhile, and among the little lambs,

Eddie, the three-year-old we lost years ago – to her but yesterday.

The poor people love her.

"She is so plain," they say, meaning natural, simple, understanding. She is plain, too, in her clothes. Hightum, her newest, well-cut coat and skirt, black, as all her clothes are – Tightum, last year's Hightum. Scrub, last year's Tightum. [These words also surface in Somerville and Ross's "Buddh Dictionary".] Her hats are very odd, too old for her, usually worn askew, trimmed – we tease her – with a wisp of net and a dead rook. But her boots and shoes and gloves are irreproachable. Indoors she wears caps, all her generation wear them, a firm velvet foundation with some kind of lace above. Stern-looking caps.

She dresses for dinner as a matter of course, in black, a square open neck back and front, elbow sleeves, sometimes a Spanish lace or Indian shawl, a lace cap on her distinguished head, beaded shoes on her long slim feet.

Her dressing-table is like her. The ivory brushes and tortoiseshell combs of her wedding dressing-bag – no wonder bristles and teeth are far from perfect – nail scissors, hand glass – or back-hair glass, as it was called, a glass hairpin box, a pincushion, a workbox, nothing more. No scents, no powder, no vanities of any kind.

OH, WHAT A DAY!

It began before six with a cheerful bustle of maids peeping in to make sure that Mother and I would be ready for our early breakfast, and in good time for the only train; and with Taylor, her head lost in my jewel-safe, counting out money for tickets, and Alice Hawkins [a housemaid, a native of Castle Freke], hurrying in to know if she looked *suitable* in her hat, because Ellen, her chief, had told her to change it for her Sunday bonnet and there wasn't time. I thought her green sailor hat suited her wide grin very well, so off she went in the wagonette to collect the company doomed to go with us to Cork. Mother and I, on the car, drove through seven miles of early sunshine, primroses and lark-song, arriving at Clonakilty half an hour before the train was to start. Close behind rumbled the wagonette.

The station-master was all agog. "Ye can wet the tea," he shouted to a hidden helper in the one small waiting-room, before assuring me that he had had my wishes attended to and breakfast was ready. "No trouble at all," he said, beaming. "'Twas a bit out of the way, but no harm in that.

The poor creatures will be in need of nourishment, leaving their homes so early, maybe without a bite or a sup."

The guard and the porter were helping them out of the wagonette; an old blind man, an old deaf woman, the nervous person – a thin middle-aged woman who is in dread that she has a fox in her innards which snatches every mouthful she swallows – and Mary-Ellen, the little fair child who is distant in her mind.

Alice knows them all, and although there were only four, she counted them twice over. She has come to shepherd them on the journey and is prepared, with the help of God, to keep them from leppin' out of the train in their fear. Not one of them has ever been in a train. They had no wish to go in a train. They had no mind to go to Cork at all. They would not be going, indeed, but for the will of God and the ladyship an' the coaxing of Miss Ha'kins (Alice).

The station-master took the deaf woman and the nervous person by the arms and settled them down to breakfast, while Alice led the trembling old man, and Mother brought Mary-Ellen, wild as a bird in her fear of the unknown, yet held by Mother's gentleness as a bird is held in the gentle hand of its captor.

"Will I bring you the tickets, me lady, or will you come to the hole in the wall?" the station-master asked. As we went I thanked him for all the trouble he had taken. "'Twas a pleasure," he said, "if onusual. Not anyone has given a party that way ever before, no, not since the railway was brought to Clon'. How many tickets will I give you?"

"Two first returns, three third returns, one and a half single."

"And would the little girl and the nervous person be left at the hospital? Would there be no hope at all for them, that they would not need return tickets, God help them? Would your ladyship wish to pay for the tickets, or will I put them on the parcels bill? 'Twould be the same in the end and leave more in hand for conveying the sick persons about Cork. Not but what there'd be pounds and pounds in your hand in any case," he added hurriedly, as I laid down the money Taylor had dealt out from the safe.

The train came in backwards with great skill. The engine driver leaped down and hurried to see what was going on in the waiting room. I heard his gentle voice encouraging the company. "Take y'r time, daddo" (Grandfather), to the blind man, "ye can't be expected to eat as fast as one who has the sight. Sure there's time enough! Haven't we the long day before us?"

"Whisht now," said the guard to the frightened child, "take a sup o' tea and have some sense."

"There'll be dollies where ye're goin'," the engine driver said to her.

"How did you get on?" I asked Alice when we reached Cork.

"They were very good, and as quiet as the dead till the train lumbered into the tunnel. Unprepared, they were, for the darkness, and never a lamp from end to end of the train." She looked reproachfully at me. I should have foreseen it.

"Mrs Sheehan (the deaf woman) was not so unruly," Alice continued, "but she cried, 'What's happened the sun an' all?' thinking it had fallen in the sea, the way it used in the old days. It was the nervous person who screamed. 'Help, Miss Ha'kins, help!' she cried, 'he have me at last.'" Alice grinned broadly. "She's all the time thinkin' of the fox and mebbe the tunnel was the fox's hole. It was the little girl was the worst, with her pinching fingers at me throat! If I'd been said by Ellen, and had put on me bonnet with its strings, the poor innocent child would have strangled me before ever I could reach the communicant's cord."

"What did the blind man say?" I asked her.

"He sat quiet. He knew no difference. 'Twas a grand journey," she went on, "thanks be to Almighty God and the guard, and the other one who kept the engine from straying off the track."

At the station we divided our forces. Alice, with the blind and deaf, left in a jingle for the "Eye-a-Near," as the people call the Eye, Ear and Throat Hospital; Mother and I to take the nervous person and the child to the "Women and Children's." Half an hour later, Mary-Ellen, a net over her cot to keep her from escaping, lay asleep with a doll as large as herself in her arms.

The nervous person was also in bed. She beckoned to me and whispered delightedly, "The docther have me examined, and 'tis a fox in me innards, he says, just as I told him. 'Why wouldn't I come before,' he asked me, 'when 'twas a small little cub? But better late than never,' he said, and on Monday morning, be the help o' God, he'll whip the red fella out o'me, an' that'll be the end of me fine gentleman."

I AND THE CHILDREN have come to England; a visit to The Pré [Mary's family home in Hertfordshire, outside St Albans] and to Mother.

When I arrived a hockey match was going on. Little girls and grown-up girls, *Grasshoppers and Scarlet Runners*, they are called. A pretty, country scene. Forty to tea. Mother has had 'flu and is still ill with a bad cough.

John is very well and audacious. He shot a sheep in the meadow with an arrow; luckily the bolt stuck in the creature's wool and did no harm. He was disappointed. Mother reproachful but proud of him; John apologetic, yet triumphant, reminding her what a saving it would have been in the housebooks had he killed it dead. "It would have done us for two weeks, *at least*," he said.

The next day he shot a number of darts into her pig. The creature bellowed and no wonder. Abrams rushed out! Papa came from the house, Mother, even, was vexed. John was surprised and pained and still more so when Papa made him give Abrams a shilling for taking the darts out. John felt that badly. "It would be more fair," he said to Papa, "if you would give me a shilling for having such a good aim!" Papa wisely took no notice.

Now I am at Folkestone by doctors' orders, here where Algy and I came after our wedding on the way to Italy and were snowed up.

Snow, and moonlight on the snow; two joyous young things, enchanted to be together for ever after, one as innocent as the other. Brother and sister looking out at the moon together in the middle of the night.

Jacky is with me, and Pidgie, my own old nanny's sister. Jacky has his tiger in his hand all day long. It is of bluish plasticine with a gigantic glass eye which he got from A.S. "My tiger," Jacky says proudly, "with a *n*uman eye."

It gets hot and soft with much caressing. Jacky loves it more than anything else because he made it himself, more or less. A.S. must have a sense of the ridiculous to put a human eye on such a monster.

I ALSO ENJOYED staying in Cambridge with Nina Hutchinson. I met Sir Robert Penrose-FitzG. there and a sympathetic Don (name forgotten) in riding clothes and blue eyes whom I had entirely forgotten altho' he swears I knew him *well*, to *talk* to – three years ago! I wonder!

Also Long Roger, still 6'5 (he swears he hasn't grown an inch since we danced through May week together four years ago), who immediately went on with a discussion about dream-control, which we dropped then, from the point at which we left it. He is very interesting and charming. Still a vegetarian and looks well on his cabbages, still the most perfect friend in the world – but not for me.

GREEN PARK CLUB, London. I am cross; nothing fits my mood. Is it because I am in town, this *wilderness of apes*? Elizadick (Canon Besley) came to tea, a beloved man, broad in build and doctrine. Today I go to Amen Court to hear him sing Imogen, my new song.

Jacky and I went by invitation to luncheon with Mr Carlyle at the Church Army Headquarters. The dining-room was in the basement – the table laid for twenty. A duchess (Adeline D. of Bedford) was there, Princess M.L. [Marie Lousie] – a doctor, a barrister, Mr Carlyle and his sister, ourselves and a dozen workers. A happy company. Jacky was much annoyed to see the places being filled up. "There won't be any room for thieves and murderers," he said. Mr Carlyle overheard and apologized for their absence.

There was some interesting talk about prisons and prisoners.

Dr J., who had lately been asked to decide if a certain criminal was sane or insane, said that far worse than the prison-cell is the prison of self from which there is no escape.

Mr C. said: "Thank God, there *is* a way of escape from self and that is by the creation of a new heart, the renewal of a right spirit; by the enlargement of sympathy the door of self is kept open."

Everyone was interested and one of the workers told us that many prisoners in solitary confinement grow very emotional. "I've learnt", he said, "in visiting them to let them do the talking – poor fellows, they get so dammed up – and to let them have their say out." An interesting thing he told us was that almost all prisoners speak with greater affection of their mothers than of their wives.

After luncheon Mr Carlyle took Jacky and me to a home for destitute men. Some of them were decidedly unattractive and Jacky kept tight hold of my hand.

I COME BACK to Castle Freke. All my garden-party neighbours come to call. I do not always feel inclined to see them but I am always "at home"; their horses go to the "visiting horses" stable to rest and feed and drink while the drivers have tea in the servants' hall, or if James McCarthy thinks them unfit for this honour, in the saddle room.

If I am out of doors and too far to be found, the callers have tea in the saloon. I shouldn't wonder if they like this better than having it with me. Some of them have driven fifteen or twenty miles.

JACKY AND I go out for a walk down to Ounahincha Strand. He is as usual full of talk about birds and beasts.

"Mike Madden says owls swallow mice whole. Do they? Why don't they chew? Do owls have tonsils and uvelars? Mike Madden says our badgers go lumberin' about at night and make the earth shake."

We arrive at the Strand. The stream, which the farmers who live round the bog divert to a new course every Bank Holiday, is back in its old bed and clattering, joyous and lively, between smooth, worn rocks, to join the sea. There is a momentary set-back when the first small sea wave meets it. They rise up together, silver and green, they sway to and fro, wave and stream, like wrestlers; the wave falls back, the bright and eager stream is merged in the great waters.

Jacky, barefooted, is busy with a home-made boat which sails broadside on and capsizes on the tiny rocks of the stream. Johnny Sweeny, passing by with fish for the "Cassle", carries him over the shingle and under the bridge to see a shoal of salmon fry.

"Oh Johnnie," I hear Jacky say, "don't you wish you were a fish? I'd like to be a flatfish lying on the bottom, looking up with my big eye to see the moon spilt on the calmness."

They settle down on the low turf wall for a prolonged talk while I, the shepherd of my memories, call up some of my flock and look them over, glad and sorrowful, and fold them there beside Ounahincha's waters of comfort.

PLUNGING INTO THE WOOD from sunshine outside. A gloom which astounds and frightens one; it is like going into the cathedral at Chartres.

As one stumbles on in the dusk, tree trunks emerge and bluebells take on their colour, the young fern fronds their tender green. A little way ahead there is a foot-wide circle of white narcissus enclosing a thirty-feet centre of moss. To follow the path one must step within the circle's magic; to escape one must take seven paces and seven more, counting aloud.

We take seven paces and if one dares to stand still every hyacinth in the wood will ring its bells, blue, pink and white will chime together; narcissi will kiss flat-face to flat face and clang like cymbals, ground ivy will rear itself to bind our feet; owls will loom onto our heads, heavy as lead, folding their hot stuffy wings over our ears and eyes, bats will cover our hands, while the ground sinks beneath our feet. So it is better not to stop.

Outside the circle, at a safe distance is a larch seat designed by Dear Man (Mr Hodson) to suit my long back and long legs. On the ground is a larch foot-rest. Little short-legged people have to sit leg-a-dangle. I seldom have short visitors; they are so awkward when we are rambling about off the roads and have to get over the demesne wall to come home.

There is a place in the wall where I usually fall, which is three feet high on the light field side with a drop of six feet into the dark wood. One slithers onto an immense pile of fallen leaves. All the same the short-legged are afraid. They balance on the top and sit and squeak until the one behind pushes them over or the one in front pulls a little leg as they fall.

When I found out that Mrs Collins and other dear old bodies always go to Mass that way I had spikes put in to make footholds for them and the Short Legs.

There is another place where we (and they) climb over, but falling is not so soft. One either slithers into the stream or one leg goes down an old fox-earth, and the other into a nettle bed.

A DELIGHTFUL THING happened to me today. An old crone gave me the blessing of Bel. "May the blessin' of Bel be upon ye."

What a bridging of the years, what a linking-up of the twentieth century with the days when Bel, the Sun-god, was worshipped in this land, in whose honour fires are still lighted upon the hills on Midsummer Eve.

The bundle of rags that was my well-wisher had no idea of the meaning of her words, so I asked another aged creature said to be a wise-woman.

"I have been blessed by Bel," I told her. "Who was Bel?"

She shuffled uneasily – "Is it Bel? ... He was one o' the Great Ones ... long ago ... an' that's all I know. 'Tis best to let them ones alone. The blessin' o' Bel is a great blessin' an' no harm can come of it but good. There don't be many left who give it and it's good luck to them who get it given them ... but the curse of Bel ..."

She shuddered and would say no more, only asking me not to tell anyone what she had said.

Later on I asked Brien, who knows of the mysteries of Bel. He seemed to think it a great good fortune for a Sassanach to receive so rare and far-reaching a blessing as that of Bel, "not but what your ladyship deserves it an' more," he added politely. Brien then taught me a most powerful and binding oath, that of Hugon, the great King of the Tuatha de Danaan (300 B.C.): "By the sun and moon, by sea and dew and colours, by all the elements, visible and invisible which are in heaven and on earth I swear ..."

"Persons", said Brien, "who break that oath, are killed by a stroke of the sun or the wind or both."

SUMMER

The cold wyndes overblowe,
And stille be the scharpe schoures,
And soudeinliche ayein his floures,
The Somer hapneth and is riche.

John Gower (?1330–1408), *Confessio Amantis*, V, ii, 75

A THUNDERING GALE! The waves are living creatures, hurling them-selves onward, furious that they cannot batter down the coast and spring upon the land to throttle and devour it. Faster and faster they come, cursing the power that holds them in leash. It is the cliffs that get the bat-tering. On the Long Strand the waves are up to the sand-hills; they seem to be playing, rushing up and rolling back with a load of sand. Tomorrow there will be a new coastline, its face covered with the exposed roots of marram grass, pale and shameful-looking.

The children go to the garden to play but Mother and I venture down to the sea. A storm with short lulls is most exciting … one can't tell what will come next … the waves dodge round both sides of the Mermaid's Rock and meet with a crash … the wind seems to blow two ways at once … we have to keep ourselves down by clutching heather stems. We are spattered with foam … breathless … the wind has swept up all the air. At last comes "a trance in the blast" when we can breathe and let go our hold of the heather. If we are wise we shall hasten away … but here is the storm upon us again; we grab at the ground with one hand and hold one anoth-er down with the other … our hats, our hairpins fly, our scarves blind us, our skirts lash round us.

A BEAUTIFUL, idle day. In London the season is in full swing. People are going round and round, all doing the same thing, on and on like processionary caterpillars whose leader's nose has been joined by some spoilsport to the tail of the hindermost. Round they creep on their little legs until exhausted, they drop down dead.

That is what would happen to me if I were in London now. Lord Barnard talked to me about it when he was here and told me I ought to go to town and "show myself" (his words). I am sure from a worldly point of view he is right, and possibly I might go if I could associate with people like those who used to come to Richmond Terrace [London S.W. 1, where Mary often stayed as a child] in the old days: the Gladstones, Granvilles, the Grays, Lord Acton, Walter Bryce, Wilfred Blunt, Arthur Godley, the old bankers Wolverton and Revelstoke, Jesuits like Father Porter, Father Morris and the saintly Father Scoles.

I have thought it well over and my answer to the world is No. I shall stay here where I have Nature, beauty and peace. I will and do share this lovely home with many people, oftenest with those whose surroundings are ugly, dull or difficult, and to whom a visit here is an unforgettable delight. Best of all Mother and my brothers and sisters will come and my dear Bellemere and my friends. This is a perfect place for the children, who could not be happier than they are. Our being here makes a vast difference to many: our own people, the "neighbours", the "poor dears", and – to M.C.

THE GREEN MEADOWS have turned gold suddenly, in a night.

"How do you like them?" the Field Angel asks, as though longing for a word of praise. "What of my enamels?"

"Gay green and glorious gold," I tell him. "But, Botticelli, my dear, won't you speckle the fields with rainbow chips as in Alpine meadows?"

He looks crestfallen and sighs. "What, here, at the Back of Beyond? Perhaps you didn't notice my red sorrel and dandelion clocks?"

Dear Angel! I wish I had not teased him. I walk gratefully through his buttercups, my shoes turning golden.

At the West Lodge I meet Johnnie Sweeny carrying a basket of green and silver mackerel, fresh from the sea.

"Will I brush your shoes, me lady?" he asks, and jerking some bracken from its stalk he kneels to his task.

"'Tis a quare thing," he murmers in his gentle voice, "the way people do always be thryin' to make a short cut to annywhere. There's yourself, me lady, wid a grand wide gravelled road an' a well-trod path thro' the wood to choose between, and yet ye come straight as a bird flies through the field, gettin' your shoes as yaller as the hair of Cleena, an' she the King of the Isle of Man's daughter. An' riskin' the onslaught of them wild young colts, anny one of them likely to destroy ye wid a shtroke of the huff. Be the same token, one day last winter, came the Reverend Mr Hodges, makin' a short cut over the bog, the gun on his arm an' him wid his head in the air lookin', please God, for a duck or a snipe ... What happened him, is it? All in a minute he was lost in the bog, swallowed up, body an' legs, an' nothin' left of him barrin' his head an' his arms, supported between two lumps of grass, be the mercy of God, an' be the chanst of his gun fallin' acrost them. There he was, wid the bog suckin', and suckin', and him shoutin' for help in a great despairin' voice ..."

"Go on, Johnnie. What happened?"

"Is it what happened him? Sure, Con Brien in the house above heard his Riverence callin' out, an' snatchin' a board from the fence an' a rope, he ran like a hare, cumbered as he was, shoutin' to encourage him, 'Hould on, yer Riverence, hould on like the divil.' Be that time there was others comin' along, farmers livin' contagious to the bog an' knowin' its tricks, leppin' be ways known to themselves. Wid the divil's uproar an' shoutin' they got his Riverence roped be the neck, he not darin' to lift a hand off the gun for fear of going under. And all the time, there was Con, straddled on the board, pulling him be the arms an' the collar of his coat, till at last, when the light was failin', an' the moon was risin', up came his Riverence from out of the bog, like it might be a person risin' from the grave ... for all the world like it might be a cork drawn from a bottle of shtout."

ON SAINT PETER'S DAY, June 29th, all the wolves in the world come together to an appointed place to meet Saint Peter. Thither he comes with a book in his hand in which are written the names of all the persons who have given themselves over to the devil, and he tells the wolves whom they are to eat.

When Peter heard this he trembled from head to foot, but God reassured him and said "Never fear, Peter, they will not harm thee; they will follow thee and listen to thy command, as if they were friendly dogs."

DOTY is coming to stay, the dear creature. She loves this place as much as I do. She was born in the nursery; her child eyes and mind learnt the meaning of loveliness from this sea, and heather, these woods and bogs.

Her heart learnt the need for love and compassion in the same cabins. She and her mother planted the white narcissi in "Paradise". It was there she learnt her catechism.

The result of these lessons is shown in her daily life. I have heard it said of her that "she has a genius for doing the right thing". She is greatly loved.

These days our padre preaches more helpfully. His sermons were always good and practical, but now he reaches the heart. This morning he spoke of genius; that of the thinker, the musician, the poet, the writer; and how in honouring them we are apt to forget that the genius which the humblest may possess, and which ranks highest with God, is that for right action; the helping hand, the cup of water,

> The little, nameless, unremembered acts
> Of kindness and of love.

I LIKE THE SOUND of raking at the front door in the early summer morning. The sun shines on the dewy grass and on the fine sea gravel, grey and a little mauve. Leaning out of an east window I see the two ancient "road men", Paddy Spillane and Ould Mike, raking out the previous day's marks of wheel and hoof.

They work diligently, keeping their withered old eyes on the ground. Then suddenly they look up, see me, and snatch off their ancient hats, genuflecting.

I feel like a statue of the Blessed Virgin framed in the window-niche.

Kitty, sleek as satin, is brought round, making hoof-marks on the smoothed gravel. She eyes me and nuzzles my neck. We set forth, two proud ladies together.

TOMMY [Sir William Young], who invited himself, has arrived! Lucia Poole has come as my chaperone.

Tommy detested her at sight and was most unfriendly to her. He is helpful to me, having examined into my money matters. He is indignant that I did not have a separate solicitor after Algy's death. Apparently I have paid large sums which should have come out of the estate.

I shall be well off, he tells me, until John comes of age. Thereafter I should have a clear thousand a year jointure besides my Cannon Brewery dividends.

I can't bear money matters, so I begin to think of other things, until Tommy thumps angrily on the table, sending my heart off into a whizz.

THE HOUSE is full of cheerful visitors. As it is Sunday, every one went to church [all upper servants and maids were Protestant], the men in black coats and top hats, and their wives in toques, very grand. Carmody and Jenkins were also in black coats and top hats. The farmers and keepers were in bowler hats, the coast-guards were in uniform, the two pews of maids all alike in their black bonnets with strings, black coats and skirts, "as pretty as pinks". The visiting maids not half so attractive as mine are, in their "ladies" made-overs. Fifty-five people. I played the organ, the singing was good and the sermon short.

Every one, after luncheon, went to the stables and garden and sea. After tea the children came down.

I was too tired to arrange how people should sit at dinner. B. [Bandon] suggested sending husbands and wives in together, binding them to be as charming to one another as they were when they were merely engaged. It was a great success. In they went,

> Tiger with tiger,
> Bear with bear,

and the flirting which went on scandalized the bewildered footmen.

The one bachelor and the one spinster took one another in and I was the odd man out. Great fun.

It was a short evening because we dined late and some of us were sleepy after the long day by and on the sea.

The Berties particularly were blind to beauty, and disparaging all things Irish. I could not allow them to know of the glory of moonlight on the sea. Because of them the moon window was curtained. There were others to whom I told the secret, making an assignation to walk on the terrace in the mystery of night's beauty, after the sleepyheads had gone to bed.

It is very seldom that I like a man and his wife equally, so that I can walk between them, arm in arm, on a wonderful night of stars. I can do this with the dear Hodsons, not being a "shadowy third" but rather, one of a trinity, for the time being.

Supposing the stars and the moon were invisible, and the night skies always a black void, would heaven have been imagined to be up above us? Probably not. Why should "ascending" seem to be more acceptable to God than descending? Why do we "lift our eyes", "lift up our hearts", "blow up the trumpet" in the new moon, "let our prayers go up like the smoke of a sacrifice"?

Why should children be told that God and Heaven are "up there"? Why should we not lay our hearts down on Earth's lap, thread prayers on the blades of grass?

TOMMY gives me a good mark now and then. "I will say for you that you aren't superstitious," he began. "No magpie, new moon, Friday, thirteen to dinner, shroud-in-the-candle nonsense about you! You don't believe in fairies, banshees, ghosts ..."

"N-no, Tommy, at least ... no, I don't believe in them, though I have seen at least two human ghosts and a dog."

"You *don't* believe in ghosts, don't be silly," he declared, fixing me with his bitter blue eye. "I suppose you know that there were no ghosts nor haunted houses until after the Reformation. They were invented by the new Protestants to make up for the loss of saints, wonder-working images and relics. In plain words, people could not do without thrills of some kind. I watched you last night when your guests began telling ghost-stories ..."

"I didn't want them to have bad nights."

"You were quite right. You were as clever as a Wagner modulation; from ghosts to reincarnation, to the amusing snobbishness of people who remember previous incarnations, to snobbish dogs, dogs generally, dogs and music ... '*Won't somebody sing?*' It was masterly."

"Thank you, Tommy. It is funny how people are sure they were kings, queens or duchesses in a previous existence. You know the B's? The daughter declares she was a maid of honour to Henrietta Maria; and the mother was the dearest friend and confidante of Charles II. '*Of course quite in a nice way,*' she told me, '*quite platonic.*' She remembers the dear King so distinctly, even the smell of his wig. He gave her a spaniel, Carlo she called it."

"Cat!" said Tommy, "You're inventing."

"I'm not. She and E. asked me what *I* was in a previous existence, so I thought I might have been a shepherd on the Berkshire downs, with a fringe of beard under his chin from ear to ear. You know, like a cut-throat."

"What did they say to that?"

"They shuddered. 'Of course,' E. said, 'you would be an *outdoor* person – but a man! A common shepherd!'"

"You never will learn sense," said Tommy. "Of course they knew you were laughing at them and they won't love you for it."

"You're wrong. They were happy looking down on me for having been a labouring man. One day when E. was being particularly uppish, I asked her if she could sit at the same table with a carpenter, a clean, gentle carpenter with washed hands?"

"Certainly not," she said, and then rather suspiciously, "What carpenter are you thinking of?"

"Jesus Christ," I said.

"One doesn't think of Him as a *carpenter*," she said reprovingly, "really, dearie, you are a little far-fetched."

MY VISITORS were sorry to go, and well they might be sorry to leave the azure sky and sea and the sunshine of this brisk day. I said I was sorry to lose them and so I was – at the time. Then,

> ... after al this nyce vanitee
> They took their leave and hoome they wenten al.

The horses were a beautiful sight at the door, all black and gleaming: Molly and Ita in the wagonette, Onaway in the car, Pegasus and Puca in the four-wheel dog-cart.

Tommy stayed behind, as he was going later, on his own to Bantry. He and I and Jacky went to the sea and while J. made a castle, Tommy and I walked up and down and talked.

He says he is a pagan, and not a Christian, which was a surprise to me. When I asked him, "What *do* you believe, then?" he said, "I believe you are a pagan, too!" which I thought very stupid of him.

He has, all the same, a devotion for St Francis and also for the Christ of his own vision, before St Paul made claims for Him, which He never made for Himself.

He loves the Psalms and some hymns and he repeated some Milton, and Tennyson's "Strong Son of God" and wrote down for me some lines by Whittier which I had not heard before. We had no paper, so he wrote them on two of those white things which Jacky calls scuttlefish's skeletons:

We may not climb the heavenly steeps
To bring the Lord Christ down;
In vain we search the lowest deeps,
For Him no depths can drown.

But warm, sweet, tender, even yet
A present help is He;
And faith has still its Olivet,
And love its Galilee.

MRS LEARY, the fish-woman, is one of our joys. Today Mabel overtook her halfway up the steep short-cut to the house. She was resting among the ferns and belated silene, her basket of fish beside her, and her eyes on four stout lobsters which were scrambling, legs and claws, towards their doom.

She got up when she saw Mabel and apologized for the path being occupied. The lobsters were heavy, she said, on top of the load of fish, so she put them out to walk the steep bit of the way.

Mabel declares that when she left them, they were going hard, neck and neck, Mrs Leary gently switching them with a bracken stalk to keep them on the course. I wish every one would kill lobsters mercifully, as we do, with a quick knife-thrust at the back of the neck.

Lobsters, Mrs Leary has taught us, have one claw for crushing and one for sawing or cutting. These are not always right and left. Mrs Leary has known lobsters to have two crushers or two saws, which must be very awkward unless they hunt in couples.

They seem to have an arrangement by which a lobster which is about to shed its out-grown shell engages a friend to guard the entrance of the cranny to which it retires for the operation and where it stays until the new shell is hard. Then it changes places with its friend.

Mrs Leary knows nothing about this, she "can't say if 'tis the thruth". She laughs shyly. "Mebbe 'tis the ladyship's fun!"

JACKY AND I often go into the wood when it rains. The trees are near together and in summer the leaves are so thick that we keep fairly dry.

Rain in the beech-wood is noisy, except when the leaves are soft and new; the sound is then much softer as if the rain fell more gently on the tender young leaves. On the great silver firs it hisses with a high-pitched sound as if the needles were whistling.

Today I drove into the wildest west to return two calls, a courtesy long overdue. The horses were put up at Glandore for a rest while I pursued my way on a hired car through glorious scenery.

As we drooled along I knew, or foreknew, that I must beware of a savage dog.

We arrived at the house; the jarvey got down and rang the bell. "Had you better get up again?" I asked him. "There – there might be a dog – a fierce dog."

He smiled indulgently, he had no fear. He rang again, and again. At last a red-eyed, swollen-faced maid came to the door.

"Is Mrs O'Connell at home?" I asked, and "Would the misthress be idden?" echoed the jarvey.

The maid shook her head and swallowed a sob.

"Mrs O'Connell kindly called on me. I am hoping to find her in," I explained encouragingly.

"Ye're too late then, ma'am," she sobbed, "the misthress is just after dyin'."

We drove away, my driver ejaculating, and obviously anxious to abandon the second call.

"'Tis not a looky day at all," he muttered, "we'd best turn back."

I pretended not to hear. "Beware of the dog!" said my Warning Angel.

I was on my guard as we drove up to the second house. The driver descended, rang the bell, and instantly out rushed a furious mastiff which bit him through his trousers in the calf.

"Let go, ye divil," he yelled, "get along out o' that. Mind yrself," he cried to me as he leaped to his seat and seized the whip.

"The young dog's a bit playful," said a man who came to the door, "a sart-av-a-butler", who was still fumbling to get rather grimy cuffs over his knuckles. "The misthress is in her bed ..."

"Begor!" whispered the jarvey, turning pale, "ye don't say there's another wan?"

The man smiled broadly. "Ye're right, Mike, an' this time 'tis a boy,

God bless him."

Luckily the bite was only a nip, as was discovered when we got to the inn at Glandore. I told James McCarthy to compensate the man.

"Would it be for the bite or for the throusers?" he asked shyly, for this was a delicate matter.

"For both," I said, and modestly retired to the roadside.

A small crowd gathered round them, fishermen, women fish-cleaners and children.

"Which leg is it?" James asked judicially.

The man felt first one and then the other. " 'Tis this leg," he cried, "but I wouldn't say which throuser the dorn dog nipped; there's holes in the both of them."

"Them holes was there last Christmas," one of the girls said, laughing. "Don't ye pay him for the throusers, sir."

"Turn them up," James ordered.

The crowd bent down like one man to see the wound, a mere bruise, and straightened again disappointed that there was no blood and mangled flesh.

"The ladyship warned me," Mike the driver said. "Ye'd best get up on the cyar," she says, when I had the bell rung. "There might be a fierce kind of a dog," she says.

He looked round at the crowd as if to say, 'tis not ivery day I drive a witch, and they all turned to stare, and to see have I the evil eye?

"How the divil did she know?" he whispered meaningly.

"Mebbe she'd been there before."

"Mebbe she'd heard of the dog."

"She had not then," the jarvey said indignantly. "Mind y'rself, I warned her, returnin' the compliment, an' there was the dog, the fine gentleman, fawnin' before her and waggin' his tail, and nivver a bark nor a bite in his mouth for her, and his own misthress above in the loft, lyin' in her bed wid a babby."

"Five shillings," said James, writhing inside his livery to get money from some secret pocket.

"'Tis too much," the crowd shouted with one voice; but the jarvey thought seven and six.

"Five shillings *and a drink*," suggested the landlord of the inn.

"Ten shillings," I said, being tired and wanting to get home.

The crowd gasped. The jarvey took off his hat, the landlord beamed.

We drove away. They had forgotten that I was a witch, and cheered.

James did not speak for some miles. Then he said suddenly, "'Twas too much." He did not speak again until we got home.

THE RAIN is coming down in spears and arrows. I can see the grass blades and the tiny flowers on the terrace quivering, bending, getting up, again and again.

As for the solitary bees which live in holes under the daisies and ladies' slippers, in company with small, solitary spiders, they must be drowning in their hundreds, God help them!

Only the worm-folk are glad. I can almost hear them cheering as they toss their heads, proud as Noah.

I AM RESTLESS, hearing the call of the road, and the call of mountains with their water courses. I must not listen. I must not leave the children to go away and away.

Jesus Christ heard the call of the road and obeyed it. If He had not been able to go here and there, He would have known the pain which comes to those who are thwarted in this respect, again and again, and He would have left some strengthening and encouraging words for those who are prisoners in their home.

Just as I am by nature restless, a mover-on, so do I want to grow, and mentally to progress; to have a wider horizon, to cross mountains and seas; glad to be beyond, glad to change; not wishing to return on my tracks; leaving by the wayside the outworn things which have served their purpose; dropping impediments; to go on in the company of those of like mind; to part from those who, like Lot's wife, look back with regret. I want to go from strength to strength, "*im Ganzen, Guten, Wahren, resolut zu leben*".

I wonder whether either of my sons will inherit my wander-thirst. If they do, I hope they will be able to satisfy it.

I have read of wander-mania taking hold of an entire tribe of African natives. *Immediately* they pick up their lion's-teeth necklaces, their clubs and assegais, the women hitch the babies on their backs, collect the goats and they all go for a "walk-about" which may last for weeks. Then, satisfied, they return to their huts.

When I told this to Tommy, he said, "Don't you believe it."

The story of Cuthman, afterwards a saint, who lived in the eighth century, and who kept his father's sheep on the Sussex downs.

So that Cuthman could go home for his dinner, his mother used to send a boy to take his place. One day the boy failed to come, so Cuthman, who must have had great faith, drew a chalk circle round the flock, saying, "*In nomine Jesu Christi, grex, tibi praecipio ne metas intra quas tibi posui ante regressum meum egrediaris.*"

The charmed sheep stayed inside the circle.

After his father's death, Cuthman's mother became paralysed and he dragged her about the county on a contraption half bed, half wheelbarrow.

They were poor by now and begging for their bread. Eventually they settled down at Steyning, where Cuthman built a hut for his mother and a Church for God.

I AM WANDERING alone in the garden, peevish, because I want to know where red rose gets her colour, and why white rose has none; whether flowers collect their fragrance from sunshine, warmth, rain, dew, or from chemicals in the earth; how roses weave their fine petals and fold them, tightly compressed, in their frail green sheath; no human pressure could fold and hold them so firmly.

How does one small seed from among the scores in one of her hips contain the life and perfection, not of one rose bush, but of millions to come? Is not life in the rose the same life that is in mankind, in me?

There is no one to answer me.

Thinking of the many glories of the borders, I wish the Lord God would walk in my garden in the cool of the evening, and would hush the eternal *how?* in me.

I would try not to ask *why?*

IT IS a most exciting summer day: a live wind, the sea all agog. But for the moon's leash it would leap ashore and carry us all away.

Jacky and Nanny and Baby and Amy, the nurserymaid, and myself are having tea on the Strand, with scalding hot tea in an iron kettle wrapped in many newspapers.

"Here's a lady's seat," Jacky says, indicating a rock. "Sit down, my dear creature, and enjoy yourself."

Baby takes off his floppy hat and sits with bare head, bald and seal-like, scrabbling his toes in the dry sand. The donkey, tied to the gate, is asleep, swaying gently in the shafts.

Battery people on their way back from a funeral at Ross pass by in their carts. The men "have drink taken". They snatch off their hats with a flourish and pass on.

Jacky and I see how unusual the sea is and how alive and splendid in its green and silver brightness.

"Was it on a day like this, do you know, that the Spanish Armada ship went down on the Dulig?" Jacky points to the black rock where the waves are tossing spray.

"No one knows. It might have been in a bright blue and white gale, or in an angry black and purple storm, or in an inky mist at night. Anyhow, the ship hurled herself on the sword of Dulig and perished."

"What a waste!" Jacky said. "Poor drowned men! How nothing they are!"

OUNAHINCHA! On a still day, if it can be said ever to be still here, when the tide is out, the winds hushed, and one's own heart beating quietly, then the voice of the little stream seems loud and important. It talks about itself to itself, hurrying the final sentences as it covers the last strip of sand. Then it is lost and silenced in the sea.

One afternoon when I was there with Jacky a sea-fog came on; it was on us before we were aware. We clutched one another's hands and ran, while we could still see, to the safety of the road and the waiting car. We hastened home followed by the climbing mist. A few minutes later the world was blotted out.

I'VE GONE AWAY again. My wits were too slow to think of a valid reason for refusing a verbal invitation. I find a garden party in full swing, a dining-room packed with company chewing cakes. People elbowing politely, walking sideways like crabs to join some acquaintance on the other side of the room. Precarious trays of black tea and pale coffee carried by harassed maids. A butting woman bangs me in the back; a kindly parson, with grimy neck and ears, smiles at me as he dives by on an errand

– tea for the Dean's lady. Bishop and Dean are here, being "charming to ladies". Ices. Peaches. Quite an orgy!

We shuffle out of the room in a solid mass, making ourselves as small as we can to get through the door. In the garden we expand and become friendly as we look at borders and beds, and walk on the shaven lawn. While people prattle, I think: here we are, imprisoned, each one of us, in a body, in solitary confinement, being given a treat; allowed to speak to other prisoners; to take exercise together. Those who can may play little games with balls; those who can't may peer into empty greenhouses, look at a young frog and a goldfish in a rockery, and talk about slugs and how to catch them, before going back to our cells.

THE TIME is twenty minutes to eight; time to change for dinner but the luggage hasn't arrived. It has been for hours at the station but the luggage-cart has to wait for the Cork train. Taylor is distracted. "It's alright," I tell her, "I can have a longer rest. I should like to have a bath!"

"What next!" Taylor thinks, "a bath in the evening!" "Anyhow, there isn't a bathroom," she says acidly.

Now she indicates sponges and brushes which came in my dressing-bag, and says I must be getting on as far as I can. I meekly get on.

At ten minutes to eight there is a bustle outside. Taylor drapes a bath towel over my shoulders and lets the luggage come in between a perspiring odd man and a finicky footman taking care of his livery.

Taylor dashes at it with a key while I undrape myself and fold the bath towel neatly on the towel rail.

My "Jay" clothes are invariably beautiful. The body in which I am pent is decked in white satin. Everything is white, stockings, shoes, lace hand-kerchief, fan, pearls, face.

A pleasant evening. I sit between my host and a shy, gentle soldier back from India. My host is very agreeable. Between soup and fish he talks about types. I seem to be, according to him, the "type" of woman he likes best, dark eyes, etc.

Between fish and entrée the woman on his right takes up the running. She also is the type he likes best. Red hair and green eyes, rather beautiful.

The soldier loves walking and tells me of walks and wild flowers in Kashmir. After dinner people sing and I play their accompaniments. I am glad I came.

J. "I wish you would wake up, Mum."

M. "I'll try to, Jacky. It is only half-past six!"

J. "I've been awake for hours. Couldn't you tell me a story? Just one or two, and then you can go to sleep again while I think if they're true."

M. "I'll tell you something I read last night about eiderducks. Mr Eiderduck is so anxious to have children that he watches beside the nest where his mate is sitting on eggs, day and night, like a policeman ..."

J. "... Or like the sentry who guards the Queen, that man with funny eyes which can only look in front."

M. "If any one comes near he warns her: Hee, Hee, Hee. Then, quickly, they cover the eggs with moss from a heap which they keep ready in case of danger. Then they creep away.

"When the danger is past, they hurry back. Sometimes Mrs Eiderduck thinks, 'Well, as I *am* off the nest, I might as well go for a walk.' So, off she goes, and then, if she stays away rather long, Mr Eiderduck comes after her in a rage and drives her back, flick-flack, with his hard, strong wings."

J. "How she would waggle from side to side to escape his wings ... running with her neck stretched out."

M. "... Then she dashes on to the eggs and sits still at once, looking innocently at the sky as if she had been on the nest all the time."

J. "She wouldn't, Mum. She'd tidy her feathers and push her eggs about. Hens do."

M. "But if she had stayed away so long that the eggs had got stone-cold before her mate could drive her back, then he would give her a great beating and leave her for good and all."

J. "I should think she'd be glad not to have him staring at her all day. But how would he know that the eggs were cold? Can he feel hot and cold with his beak or his foot? And how does he know that they won't hatch if they get cold?"

M. "It's that curious thing called instinct."

J. "I expect God told the very first eiderduck and they've been telling their children ever since, or else they've noticed for themselves. Birds do notice. A magpie notices if we don't take off our hats to it. If we do, it's a well-wisher; if we don't, it wishes us harm, like breaking our legs. Mike Madden ..."

M. "Oh, Jacky! You don't believe such nonsense!"

J. "I do, and I bow to the new moon."

M. "I'm ashamed of you!"

J. "Isn't it best to be on the safe side?"

M. "You have to find out what things are true ... all these superstitions are lies ... You can't think properly until you have cast them all out."

J. "Even unlucky Friday and spilling the salt, and thirteen at meals, and one magpie ... and ..."

M. "All nonsense, to be laughed at."

J. "Doty believes them. She's older than you, she ought to know more than you."

M. (lamely) "Doty does it for fun. She knows better."

J. "Anyhow, a magpie is a noticer. It wouldn't go into the Ark with all the other birds. It sat on the roof with its mate all the time. Noah had to climb up a ladder to feed them. If he'd let them die, God would have been furious."

M. "I don't see why a magpie is a noticer because it sat on the roof of the Ark ..."

J. "It noticed the smell inside. Wouldn't you have? Wouldn't you have sat on the roof? *Could* you have slept with monkeys?"

M. "I don't know if birds can smell."

J. "You don't know such a lot of things. I shall ask Doty."

Seven o'clock and tea, and Amy to take J. from his exhausted Mother.

A MUGGY DAY. With Jacky to the Long Strand. Many derelict starfish are lying about, sodden-looking. Jacky thinks they move along by turning on their spokes.

In the pools among the rock ledges are crimson anemones, and one of the rare green ones. They were all shut so that we could not see whether the green has turquoise eyes like the red.

Someone told me that when an anemone is large and presumably old, it sometimes loosens itself from the rock and goes for a ramble, walking on its tentacles. Stranger still, it occasionally travels about on the shell of a hermit crab. I wish I knew what keeps the crab steady while the anemone mounts. And which chooses which?

Probably the crab chooses the anemone; he gets it unstuck – somehow – from the rock, then slides it off, holds it on to a suitable shell with his arms until it has glued itself fast, then hitches the shell on to his back and walks off.

What axe has the crab to grind? Does the mounted anemone sting or frighten the crab's enemies? Is it to deceive, or for ornament?

Jacky tells me that spiders are short-sighted but they can smell well. "Just like rhinoceroses," he adds.

TRAGEDY IN GORTIGRENANE; wolves have descended on the fold. Pirates in the guise of nuns from America have taken away the flower of the flock, six flowers, six young girls, strong, healthy, "bright" and biddable, born to be mothers of healthy children.

These nuns, Irish by birth, beguiled the children with promises of happiness in this world and the next.

"'Tis Almighty God calling you, Mary Allen, calling you to be a nun. Would you give Him the go-by? God may want you to rise to be a Saint among all the other blessed Saints. The hottest place in Purgatory is kept for them who stop their ears when God calls them."

Even if I had known in time, what could I have done? I might have appealed on behalf of the parents to the Bishop of Ross, who has no great love for monks and nuns. The trouble is that the children wanted to go.

"Would ye hold me back, Mother, an' me to be the Bride of Heaven? Won't I be on me two knees prayin' for you, livin' or dead? Ah, don't be cryin' like that, Mother ..." No one could save them.

Mrs Collins, dear soul, was the saddest of the parents. I found her on the cliffs, watching for Mary's ship to go by. She had been there since early morning and she would know the ship because it was the only one sailing that day from Queenstown.

It was comforting for her to have some one near her, some one to listen to her lament. "They have gathered away Mary, me daughter, me only daughter ... they have her taken for a nun, God help her! The parting is too hard, me heart is black within me. Oh, Mary, Mary, me child, what will I do? Love of me heart, what will I do with you gone from me for ever?"

She cried a little. We talked of Mary's blue eyes and her long, golden hair. "Didn't I wash it for her every second week? Didn't I brush it for her with the little brush you gave her, it being so long an' needin' attention day by day? What will I do wid me hands them times?"

I expatiated on the good work Mary would do in the convent: the little children she would teach, the sick she would tend, the broken hearts she would bind up. The mother paid no heed. Had not the nuns said the same? She flung out her arms. "Oh, my grief! My grief on all around me! Isn't there darkness an' cloud hidin' her from me? An' me wid no father an' mother to comfort me."

She looked apologetically at me. "I go back on the ways of the past," she explained, "where was the sun shinin', an' dancin' an' singin' in the houses, an' a person had a father an' a mother livin' to bless an' comfort her. God help us in the bitter days when them an' all the world do be gone."

MISS MARY HUNGERFORD "of the Island" believes she has been insulted. Her pedigree is long and genuine. Her ancestors lie buried in their own chapel in Worcester Cathedral. "And being who I am," she gobbles, "I am asked to Castle Freke to meet people who are not gentry – even a bank clerk! ..."

"The Bishop's nephew," I murmur.

"I am surprised at you, Lady Corbery! And I shall be obliged if your butler may send for my cor (car)!"

"Of course, if you wish," I say soothingly, adding I fear mendaciously, "I was just going to ask you to come in and have tea quietly ..."

"With Lady Bandon, perhaps?" she asked, brightening.

I look hurriedly round. "I think we won't wait for Lady Bandon," I say, edging her towards the house. She walks with her haughty head in the air.

"Tea, quickly," I murmur to Carmody, who grasps the situation.

Through the window on the stairs Miss Hungerford looks over the terrace and sees Lady Bandon is deep in conversation with the bank clerk. The bank manager is standing by, waiting his turn for a word and a smile from "the lady we all love".

I hand our proud guest over to Mabel who, young as she is, has a genius for dealing with difficult people. Mabel has a delicious sense of humour and quoted this to me later:

> Of all the lunacies earth can boast,
> The one that must please the devil the most,
> Is pride reduced to the whims of terms
> Of causing the slugs to despise the worms!

The house has been full of visitors for three weeks.

Ophelia put on several pounds and looked wonderfully better. I fear Elizadick has gained a stone, or more. That is the worst of Castle Freke, it is such a hungry place. And Court's food is irresistible, for those who are here for a few days or weeks. I have no appetite, ever, but I should have less still if the food were less perfect.

Now the last guest has gone away. The one place laid in the dining-room at the shrunken table looks a poor shamed thing.

Friends are very dear and very tiring.

The farmers hereabout leave their hay week after week in large pike-cocks in the fields. I have seen it out at Christmas. Duggan tells me they have a saying:

> 'Tis time to stack the hay and carn
> When the ould doonkey blows his harn.

We have had splendid weather, however. Our hay was well-saved, a good crop.

Tonight the clouds are joining wisp by wisp together and a drop falls now and again. From the hill-top one sees the whole life of a shower: the cloud that mothers it, its coming forth and its progress across the sky, to its lovely slow ceasing in new sunshine among the heather on the cliffs.

AN AFTERNOON in Ross, "visiting". I called on Johnny, the dying nail-maker in his cabin on "the Rock"; his bed was alongside the tiny forge on which he and his forebears have made nails for 150 years. Every nail, big and little, used in the building of Castle Freke was made on this forge.

"Them were the great days," the sick man said. "They were strong and faithful nails that went yonder from here. They are houlding the timbers to this day. But now there's no call for honest nails. When there's no work a man may as well go West." His head fell back on his poor pillow and I sat still, vexed to think that we had not been buying nails from him these last few years. If I had only known!

His little old wife was quietly washing the jar in which I had brought some stewed beef. I saw her grimy finger sneak into the thick gravy. "There's life in that," she muttered, rolling the scrap of jelly on her tongue, "life as'll keep himself here another day or two for all he's been anointed."

Seeing he was asleep, we parted without words, but a clasp of the hand spoke for her. Her grey-ringed eyes were full of tears.

Father Peter Hill was in his garden and welcomed me in. We talked about many things, his sick and poor. We "unpacked our bundles of troubles", and sorted them over together. There seems so little one can do when almost every other house is a public house. We have the devil in Ross Carbery without a doubt.

"If I didn't with heart, mind and spirit, believe in the Goodness of God," said Father Peter, "there are times when I'd be surprised at Him! Well, well, we've got to have faith and not go fumbling in our dim minds trying to understand. His ways are past finding out."

We talked of Johnny Donovan who is going mad, and whether he will have to go to the asylum. "His wife, Katie, says 'No' and 'Not yet'," he said, "and cries, and Johnny cries. But if we wait we'll have her murdered under our eyes."

I went to see the Donovans. She was at her wash-tub and Johnny was sitting on the stairs, his rough, dry hair falling over a narrow forehead, his eyes flickering restlessly in his foxy face.

"What are you waiting for, Katie?" I ask her. "You are black and blue with his violence already."

She put her water-sodden hand over her mouth: "Whisht now, me lady, say nothin' until after I have him taken to the Timple. That's the 15th of August. If he isn't better after then, he can go to Cork to be set right, for it's the terror he is to me these days."

The great woman trembled all over as Johnny got up from the stairs, baring his teeth. She pushed me quickly and gently out into the street and shut the door.

Later I send James to the Barracks for a constable. Poor Katie will be vexed, but we can't have her murdered.

IN A WEEK we have the tenants and their families to tea. About 700 of them. It will be interesting. I had a small deputation before I left to beg me not to ask the Parish Priest, because he would spoil the party altogether. The people fear him and I have no reason to love Father O'Hea.

THE SANDHILLS at Castle Freke. The mystery of them, their hills and ravines, their curious round peaks and sudden single round dells, like great pot holes, wherein one lies as in a grave, seeing nothing but the sky and the larks that soar like angels to and fro between earth and heaven, and now and then a passing seagull.

The white sand trickles down as the wind sways the harsh marram grass above my head on the lip of the hollow, making a faint hissing sound. The grass is very scanty and poor, and pricks the children's bare legs. One might lie dead in one of these craters and not be found for weeks.

How alone one is under the sky, of which one sees only a little because the dell is so small and deep. The clouds pass by, driven by the wind across the blue field of heaven. I lie quiet and useless as a corpse, while outside me the world turns round, goes on. It is like being dead and in a grave that is open to the weather.

The sandhills are exquisite in their white dry purity. The wind and the rain wash them and dry them, the sun purifies and makes the thin, hard grass grow and spread to hold the dunes in their place. Under the surface the long roots run far and farther, sending up tufts of grey-green blades which stand out of the sand like swords. Here and there tiny pansies bloom, and nearer the Battery is a long drift of yellow stonecrop.

One day, walking along the sandhills from the cottage, Jacky and I and the Jenkins boys had a wonderful surprise. We were feeling deliciously frightened, for now and then we were "lost" in a ravine, or slid to the bottom of a dell and had to haul ourselves out by holding on to the grass, while the sand trickled down under our slipping feet. We had passed the old outlet from Kilkerran Lake, the outlet that marked the boundary – so I am told – of the demesne, before "Lard Jahn" changed the course of the stream, when suddenly, on the last forlorn barren hill, we came upon purple roses, low growing and sturdy and in flower.

They were of the kind that grow in the Alps; for the children they were – "*Oh! Woses!*" – for me a glorious mystery, *a finding*, a gracious gift, a delight, a secret between me and God. And somehow Algy came into the joy of it, as if he had planned a joyful surprise for me, and asked it of "One who could".

"Woses! woses! look at the woses!" the children cried, and passed on. I waited a little, and gathered them, not with my hands, but into my heart's treasury.

I couldn't stay for long, for the children were running "head in air" and just beyond was a steep sandy cliff, and at its foot the lake water running out with the tide, not deep, but deep enough to carry out the children if they fell in.

We stood on the top and looked down on the Battery ducks swimming and standing on their heads among the thousand ripples that are blue as we look at them from this side.

We slid down and crossed the bridge, the bridge which is battered down every winter by storms, and from the other side the ripples were bright gold in the light of sunset.

The children were puzzled; "Is it blue? is it gold, the water?" They wanted to take some back home in their little pails.

SUNSHINE, day after day, and a cloudless deep blue sky. The field grass and the terrace grass are parched with one great dryness. Not a mushroom to be seen nor a toadstool. There is not a fairy ring left in the land for the good Little People!

After tea I walked a dozen times up and down the terrace before going to the garden, searing my heart as I passed the scar left on the lawn where Algy's tent stood; forcing myself to look at it, hurting my heart, stabbing it with the naked fact, defying it to pity itself.

What is the use of not facing facts, even sorrow? Well, I look it in the face, a grisly thing, a lonely thing.

The only thing that helps is to ask myself what would Algy wish me to do, to think, to be? That seems all that matters, and brings me very near to him.

The rose garden is thirsty for rain! The roses look faint after the day's burning, woebegone, and pale as tired girls look going home in daylight from a May Week ball. What can be happening to brother worm and sister slug?

I HAVE BEEN desperately cross today. Miss D., the governess, gets on my nerves. She is meek and oh so stupid!

Jacky was aggravating too; he does know how to jar, that child. It is painful to have lunch day after day with a child and a governess after years of Algy's companionship. It is crushing, the absence of a man's intelligent mind and talk.

I have noticed that when one wants to cry and one refuses emotion the relief it asks for, it withdraws, and another emotion takes its place; bitterness or harshness.

One can only get relief from these, unfortunately, by a snub or harsh word. Then a third emotion comes up, vexation with oneself, remorse for having given pain or caused anger in someone else.

Up comes the wish to cry, in a vicious circle of emotions.

As I came through the trees I saw at the door two Little Sisters of the Poor. They stood there with their heads hanging down as though they were praying. They did not see me. I asked them to come in, the hot dusty little things. They had come from Cork to beg, and had left their car in Milltown. Afterwards they told me they had been praying to Saint Joseph as they stood at the door, praying that I might be kind. After a lot of pressing on my part they consented to have tea with cream.

They seemed radiantly happy as a sovereign passed into their wallet from my purse, thanks be to Saint Joseph.

Jacky was very kind to them, but when they assured him that they would pray for him, he said, "I really don't think you need! I don't want so much care taken of me! I want to be a wild man of the woods!"

The little doves were taken aback.

When they had gone I thought about them with gratitude for their healing company, and with sympathy. What have they not missed by their unnatural laws? Freedom, the love of husband and child? I hope they gain something, here or hereafter.

After tea I went to the cliffs and sat among the bracken and bell heather and sought peace of heart. Old Nell left her donkey cart and sat beside me, and what she said still haunts me. "Ye have lost the lardship, me poor ladyship, but ye have not lost everything; ye have a great deal left ... The night I got back from buryin' me husband I had not a morsel of food for me children, not a bite nor a sup to give them, and they crying for the hunger that was on them."

She held my hand; we cried for the sorrow of us all.

These poor people, I must turn to and try to help them. I am sure it would also help me.

I am so afraid of losing my memories, of having nothing to hold on to. I have not lost Algy altogether so long as I remember every little thing. But what if I were to lose both him and my memories of him?

Then said the shepherd; This is a comfortable company. You are welcome to us, for we have for the feeble as well as for the strong. Our Prince has an eye to what is done for the least of these. Come in, Mr Feeble-mind, come in, Mr Ready-to-halt; Come in, Mr Despondency and Mrs Much-afraid, his daughter.

The Pilgrim's Progress

My stony heart has gone. I feel a great wish to help the poor people round about, especially the children and the old.

There is plenty for me to do. There are my lunatic friends at the asylum. I go to see them on days when I am in Cork for organ lessons.

Last week I had a picnic lunch for forty women lunatics. I arrived with Con and there the poor things were, ready. Two or three nurses were of the party and we all shuffled off as far as we were allowed to go and sat on a bank under trees in a little field in the asylum grounds, out of sight of any buildings that might remind them of their sad lot.

The lunatics had made themselves very smart for the occasion; their hats were wonderful in colour and shape; each one wore a clean pinafore or apron with an assortment of coloured bows and a large bunch of purple phlox pinned in the middle. They were very good and Oh! so happy.

"Thompson" had sent up a wonderful tea, sugar cakes with mice on them, and plum cakes and barmbrack and bread and butter. They all had one idea, which was that I must not be allowed to get a sunstroke. One or another mounted guard over me with an open parasol, even when I sat in the shade. If I protested they all patted their heads, signed first to me and then to themselves. Do they think they are all in the asylum for sunstroke?

Mrs Leary, from Castle Freke, was there. She calls herself Lady Carbery as a rule, but when I am coming she tells the others to call her Lady Glandore.

Janie Tyner came too, the girl with whom I play duets. She was engaged to marry a curate. When he heard that her mother had died in an asylum he broke off the engagement. Janie, heartbroken, went off her head.

Here is the old dear who jabs one with a knitting needle, if one doesn't look out, and then is so sorry! Her beliefs are complicated. She believes a picture is being made of her in heaven. If she on earth is cross and jabs people with her needles, the picture will be ugly; if she is good and patient and doesn't jab, it will be lovely. When she dies she will go to heaven and she and her picture will be one.

There is a priest's sister, a very beloved woman, dark, beautiful, who knows she is "queer", and takes it as her cross and tries to show love to the rest.

One woman, the nurse told me, they dared not bring, tho' she cried and promised to be good, because on my last visit she had followed me about (I didn't know it) threatening to "send that lady west". Two nurses shadowed me all the time that day.

We talked at the picnic exactly as if it was a garden party at Castle Freke, and if one of us gave a sudden shriek or laughed at nothing, or even rolled over on the grass, no one took any notice. It was a lovely day, and no one enjoyed it more than I did; except for the kissing at the end. Lunatics, like nuns, are fond of kissing people they fancy, whether they know them well enough or not. And with lunatics one can never be quite sure that they won't bite.

Dr Woods gave leave for them to be photographed and Herr Kraft, the photographer, arrived looking quite pale. The nurses had to pose us, for when Herr Kraft approached the patients shrieked, or else wanted to kiss him. So he entrenched himself behind the camera, but it was ages before they would sit still, several of them wanting to know why he put his head in a black bag, before they consented to settle down.

THE GREAT TEA was a huge success. Nine hundred and ten people, all tenants and their families, came. The rain poured down from 12 till 2 and I could have cried for disappointment. I prayed hard instead, and no doubt 910 peple were also praying. At 2.30 the rain stopped and tho' there was no sun, the day was delightful. The grass, being short and well mown, dried up at once.

I received them all at the terrace gate, 910 handshakes and every one a hearty one. Oh, my arm and wrist and crushed fingers! Of course I had no rings on. It was lovely to see the joy of the people, their merriment and good behaviour.

John made a speech, learnt beforehand, admirably, and with good nature and friendliness. I was delighted with him and everyone so proud of him. He looked beautiful, of course.

People were enchanted with the band. I had to have a special train to get the band home at night to their barracks which cost £15 but was well worth it. How gratified every one was. They went away at 8 p.m. Another 910 handshakes.

IT IS A NIGHT of blue moonshine. September is waiting to be let in. September seems the beginning of autumn, and I do so cling to summer. It vexes me when anyone says there is a feeling of autumn in the air. It is as tactless as to say there is a dead body in the next room. It is because summer is hasting away that the beauty of this day made me feel sad. Beauty of bright blue sky and dark blue sea, and the pink-purple of the heather. A day of days! I spent a busy morning, first letters and the papers, then a revel in masses of carnations, sheafs of them, crimson, rose, pink, mauve, purple, primrose and white. Quantity and form and colour tell with mindless flowers like carnations. How unintelligent they are in their heavy beauty, compared with a tiny single dianthus, with its pretty pink fringe and its sharp little eye looking out from a glacial moraine, a little "person", trim, tiny and all there.

Then I went to church with my flowers. When I got back I found dear Reeves and Patty had arrived to luncheon. They were very friendly and stayed to tea.

After tea I drove with Jacky and Baby over the cliffs, very slowly, in the wonder of the evening; sea, sky and heather strange and lovely in a light that never was before on sea or land. Jacky had his binoculars, and reported a drifting boat, alone and empty. We were much excited, stopped and got out. Jacky produced his precious flag and tried to attract the attention of remote fishing smacks. "If they see us waving," he said, "they can't help seeing this derelict as it's between us and them." So he waved vigorously and Baby, looking important, stood with legs wide apart and signalled with his dimpled brown hands. Nothing happened! But we enjoyed the fun.

Mary Carbery

Above, the exterior of Castle Freke and its staff; below, the dining-room

Estate workers at Castle Freke: Con Brien (above left); Ned Good (above right); Jerry Spillane, Leary and Paddy Regan (below)

*Above: Arthur 'Kit' Sandford,
Mary Carbery's second husband*

*Left: A portrait of Mary with her
two eldest sons, John and Ralfe,
by Shannon*

Mary's eldest son, John, 10th Lord Carbery

Mary's third son, Christopher Sandford

AUTUMN

When we rode down Ettrick,
The day was dying, the wild birds calling
The wind was sighing, the leaves were falling
An' silent and weary, but closer thegither,
We urged our steeds thro' the faded heather
When we rode down Ettrick.

When I rode down Ettrick
The winds were shifting, the storm was waking,
The snow was drifting, my heart was breaking
For we never again were to ride thegither,
In sun or storm on the mountain heather;
When I last rode down Ettrick.

Lady John Scott (1810–1900)

ALL DAY there raged a foaming green and purple storm, with snatches of sun through scudding rags of clouds. Now the wind has fallen and the sun is setting in a golden fume. A liner crosses the sun's disc, battling with the waves, making little headway. She keeps far out, knowing what befalls her if she comes too near: Dulig's sword; Galley's fierce snout; Kinsale's butting head.

My nightmare is that one evening an American liner will run ashore on the Strand; hordes of ravenous passengers will stream up to the house. They will walk in without ringing the bell. They will demand drink and food and beds, and the Yankees will be contemptuous as there is no lift. A millionaire will sleep in my bed, while I, like the sparrow, roost upon the housetop.

THE SKY was red and the air crisp with frost. As James McCarthy drove me back from Ross Carbery today I was feeling helpless and depressed by the poverty of the people I had visited.

The cry of curlew over the bog added to my desolation.

James saw some snipe, but whether Jack or Jill he couldn't say. "'Tis a pity someone wouldn't shoot them," he said in his gentle voice.

"You wouldn't like to be shot yourself, would you?" Perhaps I looked as if I had a revolver up my sleeve, for he hurriedly assured me that he would not.

"An 'tis better to let the snipe be," he added, to conciliate me, "for there's no more mate on their bones than'd satisfy a kitten."

THERE IS at times warfare in my heart between the love for this perfect home in its lovely surroundings and the longing to wander away and away into the unknown.

So long as I live here, love of home is stronger, but when my time comes to an end, and I go forth, I feel that never, never shall I be able to send fresh roots into a strange place.

I WOKE and thought I would have a word with Bunyan. I asked him what he thought of my home.

"A stately palace, the name of which is Beautiful, standing just by the highway side."

Jacky woke up and at once demanded *Treasure Island*.

"Read it as ogrishly as you can," he ordered, "and if you can think of anything dreadfuller than Stevenson did, put it in as you go along."

Later he came in with a dead butterfly and a tumbler of water. He has discovered that with this he can make a magnifying glass.

He asks, "Why is the butterfly so small? Why isn't it as big as a bird? Why are its wings notched and why does it have white spots? Can it see us? Does it make any sort of noise, singing or humming? Does it, perhaps, but too soft for us to hear? Is it a Mr or a Mrs? Why can it run and fly when we can only run? Is it quite fair of God? Does it remember being a caterpillar? Was I anything else before I was this me? What happens when it dies? Why don't mothers know about things, *all* about them?"

TODAY I DROVE with Mabel, my sister, from Cork to Mount Desert, to lunch with "Bob" Dunscombe, a son of the Rev. Nicholas, and his family. Mrs Dunscombe might come straight out of Vanity Fair. She is unconsciously amusing and has a kind heart with an unwise tongue.

When we arrived, Mrs Bob took us upstairs to a spare bedroom and left us, saying, "Ye'll find all ye want *under the bed*!" Out of curiosity we looked under the bed and there we saw a surprising collection of objects including a sewing-machine, a hat, a bottle of cod-liver oil, the family

Bible and a tray of Bob's shirts from the wash! Luncheon was rather spoiled by Araminta the handsome daughter of the house, who contradicted and snubbed her mother whenever the poor woman spoke, and a son who glowered gloomily at his plate.

Bob was gay but very sad under the surface. Mrs Bob, for all her bright sallies, is, I should say, sadder still. They are miserably mated. Why did they marry?

Bob, delightful as ever, was full of stories of his tame otter. Mrs D interrupting with anecdotes of how the beast nips visitors' legs under the table. On this occasion it was shut up, in my honour.

IN PATRICK STREET, Cork, there is a statue to Father Mathew, the great apostle of temperance. There were also others involved in his splendid work, the pioneers, the Rev. Nicholas Dunscombe, Mr Martin, Mr Olden and Mr O'Connell. They also must not be forgotten – a parson, a Quaker, a slater and a tailor.

All honour to them. They deplored the drunkenness which ruined homes and turned good Irishmen into beasts.

All except Father Mathew were men tied to Cork by their occupations. They needed a messenger with faith and authority to preach the gospel of temperance throughout the county. They chose the one man who could work the desired miracle. On April 10th 1838 the Cork Total Abstinence Society was founded. From the beginning people flocked to join, persuaded and convinced by the priest's earnestness.

They came from Kerry and Clare, from beyond the Shannon, from the Back of Beyond and from the slums of Cork. Little did they know that it would spread over the whole of southern Ireland.

Father Mathew, astonished, decided to give his whole time to the good work. He travelled throughout Ireland holding meetings and preaching. By 1840 there were 2,530,000 members of the Total Abstinence Society.

I HAVE SPENT this middling-fine day examining and sorting the socks made by the Battery women for the Needlework Guild.

I buy the wool and pay a shilling a pair for the knitting. A pair! Except for Mary Spillane and Widow McCarthy and Katie, there isn't one of them who can make two socks the same size.

Some of the women make sharp little toes ending in a point; some make heels roomy enough for the hind claw of a gryphon. Some have huge legs with feet to fit a small boy; others no leg to speak of and feet for a giant.

Mary Spillane's socks were soft and well-shaped. She had washed the wool before she began to knit. "Och! she have the time!" the others say. Mary has no children; her neighbours pity her and secretly despise her. She is sad and a little furtive, as if she were under the shadow of God's wrath, or had been "overlooked" by a witch.

The other women have plenty of excuses. "The wool was short on me," " 'twas the heel me mother made," " 'twas me little girl that made them quare little toes," "I was waitin' for me baby to be born when I dropped the stitches, 'twas the pains …"

The wool comes from the tucking mill and smells of oil. The men like the wool left oily as it makes the socks warmer. It keeps the sea water out.

Mother, Rose and I pulled and patted and matched where we could, and twenty pairs of odd-cum-shorts have gone to Mrs Michael Bridget-Donovan's second-eldest little girl to be unravelled.

This wearisome day is over. Darkness has gripped the woods; the terrace lies in a grey-green trance; only the sea is light beyond dim sandhills and shadowy rocks.

AWAY from my dear home. Last night there was a large party and I crawled to bed at midnight, collapsed as a frost-bitten bee. At dinner I had felt myself dwindling rapidly. I thought, nothing will be left but my clothes. My satin dress will stand or kneel by its own substance, my pearls will glide down its sheeny surface and lie on the carpet with my shoes, my bony satin stays and my lace-frilled petticoat, but I shall be … other whither.

There is no doubt that people can fall in friendship, at sight, quite as easily as falling in love! The only two men, as far as I remember, who fell in friendship instantly and without words with me, as I with them, were Long Roger at Cambridge and Hillaire Belloc. H.B., sad to say, is a great friend manqué for I have never seen him from that day to this.

Long Roger and I danced and talked through a never-to-be-forgotten May Week. We were friends of the best kind. He was a few years older than I, a bachelor, a doctor, an idealist, humanitarian, and with all this he had an enchanting sense of humour and about as much imagination and poetry as I have.

But I was a young married woman, devoted to my husband. I was not sure that such a perfect friendship could last, as friendship.

When she meets a stranger, a woman, right or wrong, thinks she knows at once the sort he is. If he is not of the right sort, she lets down a shutter at the back of her eyes.

"What are you?" his eyes ask, "What are you, Face?"

And while he is probing and guessing on the threshold, the woman's eyes are already beyond the last of his defences. Or so she thinks.

I had a curious and unpleasant dream. I was outside the garden in the shrubbery, between the cork tree and the Kalmia grove. I was alone and thinking how all that part of the shrubbery is growing out of a bog, over which the roots of the trees and shrubs have made a strong surface.

Suddenly I saw "Whizzy", Willie S., and four other men whose faces I did not know. They were standing in attitudes, wearing overcoats which bulged extraordinarily, and which they clasped tightly with their hands. I stared, and they looked foolish.

"Will you tell me why you all look so funny?" I asked. "What have you got under your coats?"

They looked shyer than ever. At last "Whizzy" answered in a gruff voice, "It's our roots! We want to plant ourselves beside you."

I looked anxiously down and to my horror saw that I was rooted, deeply, strongly, in the ground. It was an awful moment!

Then I woke, and hurriedly felt for my feet.

OCTOBER. A most lovely month in Ireland, with its long twilight.

At dusk the Atlantic is a great reflector and holder of light. The cliffs are a deep indigo, the short, rough grass a dull blue. Ounahincha stream runs like molten silver through the bog, seeming in the twilight like the road to long-ago; flowing through the centuries from behind the back of beyond. Near the journey's end the stream washes the foot of the hill where three grey stones mark a King's grave. The sands are wet and shining. Over them Ounahincha pours gold and silver.

By and by the moon will make a wide path between us and Moy Mell, the island of blessed spirits.

Once in a thousand years the way is open for the souls of the dead to come home.

After a thousand years what would they with this poor, lovely land?

I think of Death as a mother calling her child to come to her. She will take off my outdoor clothes, make me tidy, then, taking my hand, will lead me quickly up a grassy bank. "Look, this is Paradise!" she will say, "Isn't it beautiful? Aren't you glad to be here?"

Samuel Rutherford writes thus about the death of a mother:

She is now above the winter, with a little change of place. Death is to her a very new thing ... so new as the first summer-rose ... or as a new paradise to a traveller broken and worn, out of breath with the sad occurrences of a long and dirty way ...

She sitteth ... meal-free, in a very considerable land which hath more than four summers in the year. Oh, what spring time is there! ... What a singing life is there! There is not a dumb bird in all that large field, but all sing.

PLOUGHING AND SOWING, haymaking, harvest, threshing, tree-planting and felling; the going forth in the morning of the labourers to work of all kinds in the fields and among the horses and cattle; the folding of sheep with their little lambs at sunset; the return to the farm of the men with carts, ploughs, scythes; the ringing of the farm bell for the third and last time at six o'clock; all these have an intense importance to one's spirit in the everyday country routine.

There is the still greater importance of sunrise and sunset, storm and fair weather, of high noon and night.

There was a silver sky today, and the fox-coloured bracken on the warren looked sultry against its brilliance. In the evening the silver turned to pink, clear and intense. Ounahincha water was a rosy ribbon crossing the brown bog. Ducks from the cottage near the bridge were playing heads and tails in the stream, white ducks flecked with the sun's colour. The lapping of the sea was the only sound; until the Mahony donkey lifted up his voice.

We also get these curious silver skies in summer. They are very dazzling and rather frightening.

THERE WAS a lonely figure plodding wearily forward, with the bent shoulders of one who carries heavy loads. He had a piece of drift wood on his arm, it might have been a cross. I walked behind him, along the wet and shining road towards the flaming west. Then I overtook him and bade him goodnight. He started and blinked and then snatched off his cap.

His thin face was good and gentle; he had blue-grey eyes and a crooked smile. "Good night, then, me lady! Ye'll forgive me that I did not know ye at wance, an' me wid the sun's gold in me eyes."

I learned that he lives beside the bo'reen which leads to St Faughna's grave.

"What do you think about as you walk along?" I asked him.

"Think, is it? 'Tis not thinkin' at all but remimberin' mostly, an' wishin' I c'd remember the many things that I've let out av me head."

A QUEEN WASP has come out of the cold into my warm room. She floated once round the flowers and now has come to rest on the table where I am writing. She is reflected in the bright wood, a pretty, golden creature, making herself very clean, rubbing her scales and her head with her legs and scraping her legs one against another. Now she is examining the room for a refuge where she can sleep through the winter. After long searching she vanishes in the deep keyhole of my bureau. I hide the key so that she shall be safe in her lodging.

What a responsible post is mine! A wasp's guardian!

It rains and it rains, the bees in the hives must be starving unless Jenkins is feeding them. No doubt the improvident queen is still laying thousands of eggs. She attends to her job, leaving the housekeeping to her workers and the weather to God.

The last swallow has gone. The terrace is covered with hundreds of little wagtails. Every autumn they come and are happy together before they go on their long journey.

So are we migrants who, when the time comes, plunge into the unknown, but less gallantly than these small birds.

IN THE AFTERNOON to the garden to mourn over frost-bitten and dying roses. I must speed them on their way and bless them for the joy they have given.

The men are tidying the great herbaceous border, where flowers continue to bloom. They have, in the end, to be cut down and the annuals thrown away so that the ground may be dug.

Old Hayes sees me looking at the lines of the fallen. "Beggin' your pardon, me lady," he says apologetically, resting on his spade, " 'twas Mr Jenkins' orders. He left this border a long time to plaze your ladyship, and annyway now 'tis time we'd put the doong down."

I have heard that the Chinese have burial places for dead flowers and a ritual for their funerals. What a lot of spare time there must be in China! I like dead flowers put away where there is earth. It hurts to see them stifling on an ash-heap or, worse than that, thrown upon a fire.

A sea-mist drifts over garden and wood. As I pass the toolshed the men are now scraping their forks and spades, thrusting them into a heap of dry sand. Then they put on their coats of white homespun flannel, to go home.

There is a lighted lamp in the Jenkins' kitchen and tea is laid for the four of them. The scent of hot scones bores thro' the mist. "Good-night," I call to them, and make for home, floundering a little where the wood ends and the road is lost in the fog.

It has been a cindery day! Accounts. Many interruptions. "A world of household matters filled her mind."

Carmody is at the hall door, mist pearls in his long whiskers. He looks reprovingly at me. A shadow veers away from the door. It is the good Jenkins, who unbeknownst has been shepherding me into safety.

THERE WAS an afternoon long ago now when Algy drove me to pay a sick-call in a cabin up a bo'reen, under a rocky, heathery hill. The bo'reen was too narrow for the pony cart to turn, so he stopped at the crossroads for me to get out. Suddenly I was afraid. "I can't, I know I shall meet a bull!"

Algy laughed, so reluctantly I got down and walked fifty yards further.

The lane had a twist in it. Going round the bend I saw the bull, twenty feet away, standing on his hind legs and eating leaves on the hedge which topped the bank.

A piece of rope trailed from the halter round his neck. Fortunately he did not see me. The bend in the lane hid me as I rapidly retreated.

I explained to Algy and at first he did not believe me. But I had hardly got back into the pony cart before the bull appeared round the corner. Racing after him came the gossoon who had allowed him to stray. "Get along out o' that!" he shouted, grabbing the rope and turning him round. He seemed to be on good terms with the snorting beast. We called the bo'reen "the twisty bull's lane" after that episode.

I went back there alone this afternoon to see a man who is dying of cancer. He has been a savage father to his children and a brutal husband to his excellent wife. Again and again he turned the poor woman out into the night, barefooted, with nothing on but her night-gown. Sometimes when she stood knocking on the window pane, he would sharpen a knife in her sight and rush with it into the bedroom. As he had often threatened to kill her and the children, her agony may be imagined. By and by he would come out, grinning diabolically, to drag her into the house. He tortured her, but actually stopped short at murder.

Now he is scared at the thought of death and purgatory. He is not surly any more and has grown to love his family. He has confessed his sins and been absolved; has been anointed and is waiting for death.

I find him lying on his bed with his face to the wall; his wife sitting beside him, patting him gently as one pats a baby.

"I do be tellin' him that I forgive him everything," she murmers, "and sure Almighty God willn't be harsh wid the poor little fella."

When I come out from the cabin the sun is setting, bringing the lovely autumn day to a golden end. On the sheltered bank in the lane there still are flowers; blue sheep's bit (scabious) and the fairy harebell.

Tiny blue butterflies are flitting about the flowers, sipping the last sweet nectar of the year.

IT HAS BEEN SAID that there is no greater bore than he who tells his dreams at breakfast. I am sure that is true and that dreams are private matters best kept to ourselves. Dreams, we are told, are nonsense, and to pay attention to a dream is to be superstitious. All the same, the world would be much poorer if Jacob had not told his dream. His ladder is a beautiful vision, and not only for children. It makes Heaven more accessible.

As a child I believed that the way to Heaven is by a moon-path over the sea. I greatly dreaded dying on a moonless night. A ladder that is always set up between Heaven and Earth, dangerous as my fearful mind imagined it, would be at hand, moon or no moon, with ascending angels to give one a lift. And Joseph's dream of his brethren's sheaves bowing down to his sheaf has helped many a younger child, depressed by a sense of inferiority.

Some of my dreams have had great influence on my life, and these I am going to set down, although I do not think there is any fear of my forgetting them.

The first came to me in 1892 when Algy and I were living in a villa at El Biar above Algiers. I saw my mother in the utmost distress and my brother Philip, then about six years old, also unhappy. Both of them were crying. Normally, loving them both so much, I should have gone up to them to share their grief and try to comfort them. But it seemed that I had died, and was in my intangible immortal body.

I stood beside another spirit, that of my mother's sister Mary Bonham. With a new, a greater love, we looked at the two unhappy ones; then we turned to one another and smiled. We knew the wherefore of their grief, that this sorrow was as the pruning of a rose tree and that the soul's roses would be more beautiful for the pain.

Another dream. I was on a long straight dreary road, dusty, trodden by many feet. It was lost in a sad flat distance. Many pilgrims were plodding along the road in silence. Then I noticed that by the side of the road was a slender tower like an Irish round tower. Perhaps six feet in diameter, it reached up into the clouds. There was no door. Through an arch I saw a spiral staircase leading up towards the invisible summit of the tower, lost in the clouds. I was impelled to go in. And then I noticed that a few feet above ground level a room jutted out from the tower. It was very small, perhaps five feet square and about ten feet high. Raised on two steps was a wooden cross. I knew that the wide world could not hold anything of greater moment.

I stood in the entrance and dared not look at That which hung upon the cross. I could not look above the bleeding feet. As I stood there trembling and afraid, a voice from behind me said, "You must look." Still I was afraid. Then again I heard stern words, "You must look on Him who died that we may live."

At last I looked. I saw the agony of His death. And there was nothing that I could do.

In another dream I went casually into my sitting-room and was not particularly surprised to see an angel sitting in the west window, working at an embroidery frame. One hand above, one hand below, and his needle going busily in and out. He was not my guardian angel, whose face I know quite well, but a stranger. He wore a long coat of grey frieze which might have been woven by Hayes the weaver, in Ross Carbery. I did not see his wings.

"Good morning," I said. "I am glad you have come here to work; what lovely colours you are using!"

"And what lovely colours," he answered, "there are in the view from this window. It would be hard to match the blues and greens in the sea today."

I noticed that he was threading his needle with black silk.

"Black?" I asked. "Won't that spoil your embroidery?"

"I will show you," he said. "Wait while I unroll it."

I noticed then that the work he had already done was carefully rolled up with tissue paper and pins, like any old maid's worsted work. He spread it out and I bent over him and saw an unimaginably beautiful panel of leaves and flowers, flowers such as one only sees in dreams.

As I looked he pointed with his needle to the touches of black silk which made the flowers stand out from the background.

"As you see, the design would be nothing without those few black stitches," he said. I could see that this was true.

"What is it?" I asked him, feeling sure that angels would not embroider counterpanes or cushion covers, or even altar cloths.

"It is for you," he said, "it is your Web of Life. The black stitches are sorrows that must come."

Years passed before I met this angel again. This time he held a bright and many-coloured object in his hand. It was beautiful and seemed alive.

"By the bye," he said to me, "what have you done with your bit of the rainbow?"

"I have it quite safe, wrapped in cotton wool, in my dressing-case. It is as beautiful as ever it was," I said eagerly, although in my heart I felt a sudden dismay, remembering the story of the talent wrapped in the napkin.

"H'm," said the angel, "how often have you matched it?"

"Matched it?"

"With other people's bits?" he said.

"Oh, misery!" I cried, "I see it all now! I have not gone about enough among people. I never thought about matching my bits with theirs. I am so sorry, Angel."

He looked at me thoughtfully. "I shouldn't worry," he said kindly, "I dare say you were right. It might have got tarnished."

Here is one of the wild nightmares of an expectant mother. I dreamed it in 1892, before my first baby was born. In this dream the Inquisition was in Ross Carbery. The Inquisitors sat in the Courthouse. I was brought before them by Walsh the saddler, known as the Mayor of Ross, in his white working apron, and his kind every day face was beaming upon me.

"Ye'd best be said by them," he whispered, jerking his thumb towards my judges as he led me in.

The Inquisitors were in full fig of mitres and copes. I normally have friendly feeling towards the Church of Rome, but in spite of this, the blood of my English Protestant forebears and my Scottish Presbyterian forebears rose up in me. I listened to my judges as they spoke solemnly and kindly, warning me to abjure my errors, join the Church of Rome, and thus save my soul.

"No," I answered, "never! I would rather be burnt!"

I saw Walsh looking sorrowfully at me from the door.

"Is that your last word?" asked one of the Inquisitors.

"My first, my last, my only word is no!"

Just then I saw my dear mother-in-law beckoning to me from a side door.

"Can I go for a minute?" I asked the Court.

"Certainly, and listen well to the advice she gives you."

"Follow my example," she whispered.

"I will, I will, dearest," I answered, "we will go to the stake together."

"Not at all," she said. "It would be a foolish and wasteful thing to allow ourselves to be burnt. Turn atheist as I have done. It is only Protestants they burn."

I was aghast. One of my dearest idols had crashed to the ground.

My mother-in-law went out with strange skips and bounds as I turned back to learn my fate.

The Inquisitors seemed embarrassed. Michael Walsh was talking to them in a gabbling voice. The Chief Inquisitor beckoned me to come near and handed me a slip of paper. On it was written: "We regret your blindness and your obstinacy. We pity you for your foolish courage. We should have been obliged to burn you at the stake. However, you are expecting a child. That being the case, you are reprieved. We shall pray for your conversion."

Curiously, my first feeling on waking was disappointment! I have always had a great admiration for martyrs. My second feeling was horror that I could have dreamt so untruly and disloyally about my dear Bellemère.

ALL SOULS DAY. This has been a day of restless weather, clouds scudding across a grey sky, sudden rain storms, and in the trees a sorrowful wind sighing and moaning. All Souls, good and bad, for whom Christ died. There must be a great company of them for whom no mortal ever breathes or has breathed one prayer, and though I can't persuade myself that my prayers could make any difference to the fate of souls "in the hand of God", in my earth-heart I am sure that they are less lonely for knowing that someone remembers and cares.

It is usual to pray for "the faithful departed". But who prays for the unfaithful dead, the ignorant, the untaught? Who prays for the repose of the soul of Oliver Cromwell, Byron or Robespierre, of Richard III, Queen Elizabeth or Dick Turpin?

Even though on this day in Paris, mass is said for the repose of the soul of Henry VIII in Notre Dame.

In a momentary lull, I imagine the shore-drifting men, newly drowned, crying for mercy.

In the depths is peace. There the old drowned lie quiet, barnacles on their bones, green weed on their skulls.

I seem to lie among them, turning my apathetic eyes towards the tumbling surface far above, dull eyes, the colour of green anemones. Not long drowned.

The Dead, most of them, are forgotten as soon as the last of those who knew and loved them dies. After that they are names about which may hang shreds of tradition. When the names have faded from deeds and registers or been worn away by weather and time from tombstones, the obliteration is complete. But then, lost as individuals, they live again as forebears, family, clan, people, or as hunters, warriors, saints.

The night is dark; the crying of the wind grows more and more piteous, like the cry of lost and frightened children.

Oh peace, peace be to you, all Souls.

I HAVE BEEN staying on Gigha and was glad to get away from it although the FitzRoys and Harry were so kind. Islands don't suit my claustrophobic nature.

Now Jacky and I are staying at Douglas-Support near Glasgow with the Bats (Sholto-Douglases). From my window I see a garden of terraces and yew hedges. The house is fine, with Adam interior, comfortable and cheerful, and no doubt full of angels.

The Bats are attractive in their goodness, though very Pi. They aren't too good to have a first-rate cook and comforts. How wise they are. If one's body is warmed and fed, one's mind and spirits can behave and work twice as well.

Violet Bat has a furious cold and lies in a carved Elizabethan bed. Such a lovely day wasted, with early frost, gossamers, sunshine, and I sitting beside her, while she talks Pi-talk! She gives Good Advice! She says I am much aged in appearance. True, Mrs Bat. And they would like to come to Castle Freke for a mission and to stay ten days (sea air).

"It will be good for all of you there to be shaken up a bit, spiritually."

"Yes, of course, Violet!" I dare say this plan won't materialize.

I have escaped to my room, with tears springing up because I feel that there lies under Violet's goodness and kindness a sort of malevolence, or is it jealousy of my youth? Or what?

And then to have wasted the lovely morning indoors that never will come again, never.

SOMETIMES fear grips me by the throat, not of people or what they may do, but of the force, the inevitableness and pitilessness of life. It isn't all the time, very seldom in fact, and it is usually when I am cheerful and busy.

Perhaps it is the bony finger of some puritan ancestor, jealous of joy. Perhaps it is because Algy is not here to protect me. But, when the thing springs, I struggle madly, appealing with all my soul to God, who is stronger than fate.

It isn't premonition of anything in particular. It is, I imagine, sheer subconscious dread of the ultimate solitariness of life, and because one part of me knows, or remembers, that somewhere there is safety, stability, and no such thing as fear.

> East and west upon the people I becke,
> As doth a dove sitting upon a barn.
> *The Pardoner's Tale (Chaucer)*

THE BATS are coming to stay. They propose to hold a mission, preaching in four or five neighbouring parishes.

They have heard that people in the south of Ireland are "lukewarm". I am to go from house to house and prepare the way before them. I might as well do that as anything else, but first I must ask leave of our Rector Mr Hodges and of the Bishop.

Mr Hodges is very pleased about it; but the Bishop is worried. He doesn't like missions, feeling that they often lead to emotion and excitement. He is greatly surprised that I should suggest so notoriously Evangelical a clergyman as Mr Sholto-Douglas. He had heard that I am an advanced Ritualist, etc. etc. but he doesn't refuse, and I write him a nice letter and assure him that I have never been "high church".

I drive every afternoon to ask Protestant people to come. Some will, some won't. The latter are no doubt afraid there will be collections. Amongst those who are coming, one dear creature in a wig claps her hands for joy! "Well, now, isn't that grand! 'Tis the surprise of me life to find that you are on the Lord's side!"

Whose side does she think me to be on?

First day. The Bats arrived tired and cross. They felt better after a late luncheon, rest, an early tea and a first-rate dinner, but they were annoyed because I do not have evening prayers.

We talked over arrangements for the mission. They were anxious to know if I had asked some "sinners" to stay in the house (persons in need of help, they call them). I don't know any sinners, but I wire to Jane (a good wife and mother), and to Hewett Poole and his sister, excellent people who can be relied on to help me all they can, and to Patty Reeves who likes staying here, and to Arthur Sandford.

Second day. I rode Kitty as usual from 8.00 to 8.45; a most lovely day. Magnificat.

A scurry to change and be down for prayers at 9.00. I let Bat say a few words. Jacky, in a loud voice to me at 9.10: "How much longer must we pray? I shall be late for lessons."

After I have seen Court about meals (Bat is a gourmet), the missioners try to entice me into the drawing-room.

"I'm so sorry, I must go to the nursery."

"Well, after that?"

"I want you to come for a drive. I have to visit a sick woman."

"We stay in to study the Word of God."

I dash up and collect Nanny and Baby to drive with me. We go to the Strand where I deposit them. Then I drive up the twisty Bull's lane to see Con Brien's sick mother. I notice Jerome's cheek and neck have gone crimson though he says nothing. I look round. There is old Mrs Brien sitting on a wooden chair outside the door of her cottage, stark naked!

"Will I go get Con?" mutters Jerome, and I think that a good plan. Con is her son.

"Faix, 'tis me ladyship," says Con's mother, getting up and curtseying. She looks very ill. "Will ye take a seat on the wall? Meself must sit in the chair till me son gets back. I can get no rest at all, at all 'iddin (within)."

"And why not? You'll get your death of cold sitting out here."

"Then 'tis me death I will get, as I was tellin' the priest when he said I'd be taken ayst to the 'sylum. What's wrong wid me, I'd like to know? Can ye tell me what's wrong wid me to make his Reverence talk so wild?"

"We'll talk about it when we get you dressed," I said, hoping to coax her indoors.

"Is it dressed? Amn't I dressed as God made me an' me hair wid the little pins to keep it up, God help us?"

"Ah, ah," she shrieked, "would ye put that ould thing over me head?" seeing me advancing upon her holding a petticoat and shawl which lay across the threshold. "If 'twas yer own purty coat it'ud be different."

I heard the car returning and stopping at the bend of the lane. Then Con's steps.

"Here then," I said in desperation, and put her skinny arms into my homespun coat which came to her knees, "Now, how's that?"

"'Tis fine then, fine enough for the Mother of God, an' hot as hell from the warmth of yer body! Look at that, now," she said to her son, "You and the priest tuk ivery stitch av me clothes from me, an' see what the ladyship's give me. Look you well at it!"

So saying, she whipped the coat off, threw it at poor shamed Con and fell backwards again on the chair. He hastened indoors for a blanket, which he held forcibly round her.

" 'Tis six times and seven times I have her dressed this marnin', for she wouldn't keep to the bed as the docther said." His blue eyes filled with tears. "She tears the clothes off her as fast as I put them on! What ever will I do with the poor crayther, and she the clane, dacent, honest woman all her life? Whist, mother, whist," he said, as she struggled, "'tis to your bed I'll be carryin' ye." He put his strong arms round her frail old body.

"'Tis the good son ye are to yer ould mother, avick," she said, suddenly tired, and putting her head on his shoulder. "Ye can dress me now, Connie," she murmured, as he laid her down in the inner room, "An' 'tis the death clothes ye can put on me, for I'll niver leave the bed alive."

Her face was very white and her eyes shut slowly. "Shall Jerome go for the doctor?" I asked, "Or for the priest?"

"There's no need," he said, his eyes on her face, "She was anointed three days ago when she tuk ill, and the docther said there was naught he cud do. 'Tis her heart that's worn out. I ask your pardon, me lady, for her behavin' as she did, and me back not turned on her five minyutes."

I ran down the lane to the car where, in the well, there was always a box of what Jerome called the "Rimidies", and went back with brandy. She was asleep, spent by her fighting. I put another blanket over her and heated some milk in the wood embers. Con sat, his elbow on his knee, looking at her.

"Can I be let stay wid her?" he whispered, " 'tis the last time, mebbe."

"Of course, Con, of course."

I left him there, and picking up Baby and Nanny returned to my guests. The Bats were cold and aloof. I had "turned my back on the Word of God". I did not tell them how my morning had been spent. In the afternoon and evening we had services.

Con's mother died at sunset. He came to tell me, just as we finished dinner, standing at the open door, tall, gaunt, the moon gilding his face and his short beard. He had taken off his rush hat and held it between him and the moon.

"The ould woman," he said, but with no disrespect, "she have gone wesht. She went wid the turn o' the tide, an' as quiet."

"You will miss her, Con," I said to him. "She was a good mother and you have been the best of sons to her. You went all the way with her."

"I did so," he murmured. "I did so, be the help of God. An' now to the priest I must be goin'. Good night, me Lady, and God's blessing on you."

He trudged off on his three-mile walk, limping a little.

I went back to the Bats. They were angry because I absolutely refused to ask Roman Catholics to come to the meetings or secretly to the house.

Mr Hodges backed me up. Behind their backs he looked at me rather roguishly.

The Bats expect me to go with them to every meeting, two a day, at 3.00 and at 7.00. We are to have a solid tea, and hot supper on our return.

They pity me for having a rector "whose eyes are darkened". Why do they judge people? They little know what a good life he leads.

Upstairs, I open my west window. Across the quiet sea lies the golden path to Moy Mell.

Con, returning to his desolate home, will see it and be glad.

Third day. Wind and rain. I forego my ride and stay longer in bed, pondering on Bat's sermon. I like his preaching better than his dictatorial, extempore prayers.

Fourth day. To the garden with my very dear friend J. She has been at Bat's service and was smitten to the heart by the sermon. She cried, as we sat under the old ilex, because she had not begun to live for God in her youth. She feared it was now too late.

Fifth day. Saturday. I felt too strung up to sleep, so having John Donne at hand, I consulted him about preaching like the Bat's. John Donne defended him:

The preacher maketh a holy noise in the conscience of the congregation, and when he hath awakened them ... he casts some claps of thunder, some intimidations in denouncing the judgements of God, and he flings open the Gates of Heaven that they may hear, and look up and see a man sent by God, with power to infuse his fear upon them.

Arthur Sandford and Hewett P. came today, too late to attend the services. A special "talk" has been arranged for them for tomorrow, Sunday, after tea. They will "attend Divine Worship" in the morning. A.S. has brought his topper. H.P. started with his, but it never got here. It may have gone to Skibbereen, Courtmacsherry or Bantry. Or it may have fallen off the luggage cart in which case a word from the priest will make the finder bring it here.

Seventh day. Monday. The Bats have gone. I am worn out, but thankful to have reached the end of the Mission. The Bats have no idea of how hard we all worked, padres and people, to give them satisfaction. They were dissatisfied because they had roped in no Roman Catholics. They were angry with Hewett Poole and Arthur Sandford who asked them inconvenient questions about miracles, etc.

At the last they caught me, and asked "for a few words". They had discovered my besetting sin! I am obsessed by Nature. I am too much out of doors (that means my early morning ride). I deliberately reject opportunities of studying the Word with those who can teach it, in order to be out. I am little better than a Pagan!

I listen meekly, inwardly raging. Haven't I been to eight out of ten services, *twelve hours* of listening to these missionaries? Have I not been stirred and even made to weep by Bat's lurid sermons? Have I not honestly examined into my life?

I say nothing. Luckily for me, Carmody comes in with his watch in his hand. They depart.

The Bats left me with a number of points of advice, which they ordered me to think over.

1. It is lawful to sleep, and eat.

2. I may be a Martha in my house, "looking well to the ways of her household". (Violet Bat says her room here was not properly dusted.)

3. I must study the Scriptures.

4. I must attend and even hold "meetings".

5. I may read *The Christian* and other Evangelical papers, lives of missionaries, pseudo-scientific books on the Geology of the Bible, etc.

6. I must have regular times for prayer.

7. I may attend to worldly matters like investments, pass-books, etc.

8. I can go to parties in Godly houses.

9. In visiting the Roman Catholic sick and poor, I must not fail to give them tracts. In fact, I must be a missionary to papists.

After consideration, I think the scheme will work in parts; but not on fine days.

The outdoor spirit is hostile to indoors, domesticity, duty, love and home-making. It is hostile to houses and churches and theatres and railway trains and business. It is apt to leave sick people and those who have given birth to children. It hates clothes that spoil with weather and finery and grandeur.

It is simple and clean. It lives in and with and for God and for itself, God's child. It turns people from their purpose and makes them forget what it is they want.

It may make them daft and helpless and of no account among their fellow men.

In marriage, unless the two are soul-lovers, it comes to grief. It grows sad, and becomes mortal, an orphan, and better dead.

Milton would have had a word to say in my defence:

In those vernal seasons of the year, when the air is calm and pleasant,
it were an injury and sullenness against Nature, not to go out and see
her riches and partake in her rejoicing with Heaven and Earth.

Then he would have said to me, aside, of Bat, "He is a true wayfaring Christian."

Mohammed says:

Whoever believes in God and the Resurrection must respect his guest; and the time of his being kind to him is one day and one night and the period of entertaining him is three days and after that, if he does it longer, it benefits him more, but it is not right for a guest to stay in the house longer than three days.

I HAD AN EXPERIENCE once, when I had gas, a vision in the dentist's chair with my face in a rubber bag, of my light soul passing through vast layers of rainbow colour, with a slight solidity against which I pressed in my eager going forward, and which kept me from too great haste.

I passed from crimson that was almost black, and rose colour and pink, through amethyst and sapphire and turquoise to jade and emerald green, to topaz, to pure gold, to primrose and so to whiteness so dazzling that I knew it to be the great white throne of God.

And with that whiteness in my mind I woke to earth, to the dentist and the doctor, and the life of the body.

TAEDIUM VITAE ... I imagine this comes only when one has no definite work to do, when one is idle and without purpose.

Possibly why I find some people so difficult is because most of them, and certainly myself, are not working, and even are not conscious of the need for working for or at something with a purpose *beyond the needs of the world.*

The routine that has to be got through should not be the end of life, but be only the equipment that enables us to do better the enduring work.

The Church Army and Salvation Army seem to work like this. They live simply, with plain uniform, simple food, no luxury. This part of their life is insignificant and takes very little time or thought. So much is gained for the real work; strength, attention, time.

Their object: to share the light and joy that they have with others who are without it. They lift, cleanse, heal, strengthen; they share that which they believe survives the life of the body. They succour the body to develop the soul and in doing this find peace and life in the spiritual sense.

They have not much time for intellectual pursuits. Art is not for them. They seldom have perception of natural beauty.

There are too few of them for the numbers of derelicts needing their care.

Christ knew the need. He was never rushed or overworked or fussed. He went for walks, sat in gardens and on the mountains, visited his friends, supped, slept, and went for sails on the lake.

His was an ideal life and far better than one occupied in incessant work, even good work.

WHEN SEA-FOG comes on suddenly, what happens to larks singing in sunshine overhead?

Do they fall in terror with mist blinding their eyes, and the descending song stifled in their throats?

Do they crash on the ground or do they sense it in time to slacken their speed?

Do the gulls fall into the sea or do they crouch on the cliffs for hours and hours?

Do sea birds drink sea water? Their raucous voices are heard above the thunder of sea and wind.

There are little white gulls (tern) at the waves' edge at high tide, searching for little fish, chattering with their harsh little voices.

After a dive, cormorants on the sea rocks stretch, body and neck, shaking their wings, sitting for a little like carved heraldic birds, before diving again, propelling themselves under water by their great webbed feet, coming up at an incredible distance to breathe, and to swallow their miserable prey.

I talked today with Brien about Fairy Music. He told me of "fairy harps in the rath on the hill. The weeshy harper wid hair and beard white as the bog cotton ... the weeshy harp of black bog-oak with gold laid in the wood, an' silver wires to the harp. The harper plucking the wires with weeshy hands like the hands of a mole ... an' wearin' a green wrapper wid throusers of weasel-skin and silver shoon that stamp wid the tune.

"There's the other one that blows the pipes an' the little fella wid the drum, an' Them that dances and cheers at the end of the party, the quare sharp sound like the cry of a rabbit an' him torturin' in the trap."

"And who has seen all this and lived, Brien?" I asked.

He was very grave. " 'Tis only them that has the good heart an' that has no love for gold, nor any love for the dhrink. They're none of them left now, the seein' folk! Persons do be more wishful for porter in these days."

I DREAMT of walking in a thin wood of silver birch, and of coming upon a shallow pool of inky water, whose surface was painted with gold leaves, a sun-touched splash of gold on a magic pool. Beyond were three rowan trees, still red with berries, and a white, sandy lane. "This must be Lagandarroch Wood," I said, and wondered how I had come to Scotland. It isn't often that one finds oneself in a poem, but that is where I was.

> I wonder is there any place on earth so good
> As Lagandarroch Wood?
> For just below the warm grey rocks where still
> Gold mist of scattered birches climb the hill,
> There flames a little rowan tree, well loved by me,
> Which every Autumn signals up the glen
> To tired returning shepherd men,
> Telling of hearth and home, of food and fire,
> And all God's full response to man's desire.

TODAY I looked over souvenirs of the admirers of my youth. In those days, ten years ago, we called them lovers. The name had not then been desecrated.

Valentines, love-letters, poems (of sorts), cotillion favours, ball-programmes, withered flowers.

The flowers seem to mean more than all the rest and I kissed each one as I dropped it in the fire. I read the letters, simple, direct, young and good as we all were. I stood up their photographs and wondered at their different faces, and why each one had believed me to be his twin soul and only woman. I thanked them for the honour they did me.

Then I burnt the lot – without regret.

WINTER

Beginne from first, where he encradled was
In simple cratch, wrapt in a wad of hay,
Betweene the toylefull oxe and humble Asse,
And in what rags, and in how base aray,
The glory of our heavenly riches lay,
When him the silly Shepheards came to see,
Whom greatest Princes sought on lowest knee.

Edmund Spenser (?1552–99), 'An Hymne of Heavenly Love'

OUR WINTER GALES rage usually for three days together; they are wild and noisy; I realize the splendour of them and am not angered by the turmoil. At night, when at last the wind falls, the silence wakes me.

AT ONE END of the saloon there is a wide hearth and a fire which never goes out. Great logs of beech, sycamore and oak lie on a bed of white ashes which accumulate from year to year.

Today as I came down the stairs for my Irish lesson, I saw Brien stooping over the hearth examining something with attention. He jumped when I spoke and turned round, his face red and a little sheepish.

"I was looking at the quare little marks on the ashes," he explained. "Ye'd say they'd be weeshy footprints, there, where the ashes are shallow."

"Would it be mice, do you think?" I asked, but feeling sure that we harbour no such things.

"Mebbe 'tis mice," he answered, "unless it would be …"

"But, do you believe in fai— in the Little People?"

"I would not say that I believe in them," he answered seriously. "All the same I would not deny that I have heard their music comin' out of the hill behind me own farm. 'Tis well known that they have a shefro (fairy house) in that hill."

Seeing that I was as serious as himself he went on, "If ye would hear their music for y'rself, I would lead you, next full moon, to the very spot. There would no harm overtake ye, for They'd know the respect ye have for them and the likin' ye have for the shanacha – the ould knowledge of the past."

"All the same they might not care to play for a Sassenach! What is it like, their music?"

" 'Tis not always the same. When I was a small little lad I heard their whistlin' and chirpin' many a time out of the hill and the tappin' of dancin' feet, no more than that. But not so very long ago, I was returnin' from Ardfield be the light o' the moon, when a mist rose out of the sea, blindin' me eyes so that there was nothin' for it but to sit down where I was, not a cock's stride from the hill of the shefro.

" 'Twas a quare thing happened to me, a feelin' that ever'thing in the world had come to rest, an' time, like a drunken man, after reelin' this way an' that way between the Creation of the World an' the Day of Judgment, was come to a stop, like the drunken man rolled into a ditch and lyin' there onconscious.

" 'Twas then the music struck on me through the mist, the fiddles, soundin' like a man hummin' through his nose, the screech o' the whistles, the roarin' and bellowin' o' pipes and the rollin' o' parchmint drums. Och, 'twas grand! And I felt no surprise nor yet fear; I was as much at me aise as was the man in the ditch, lost to the trouble of the world."

"Were they playing any tune you knew?"

"Mebbe the fiddles were playin' 'The Fox's Sleep', and them twiddlin' whistles tryin' for 'The Twistin' of the Rope', but the pipes and drums was like the thunderin' and ragin' of a storm, or the battlin' of rebellious angels thrown out of Heaven."

"Were you there all night?"

"I'd find it hard to say how long I was there, wid time suspended like him in the ditch. Anyway, after a bit the mist rolled away, the moon shone, and sidh-geehy (a fairy wind, pronounced shee-geehy) began to blow from the hill, sendin' me hat flyin' an' me after it, followed by the laughter of the Little People."

"I expect their laughter was like the chiming of that clock. Listen."

Brien listened. " 'Twas not at all like the clock," he said. " 'Twas more like the joyful cacklin' of a hen, or the cracklin' of thorns under the bastable."

Brien planned now to take me deeper into fairy lore, and produced a semi-transparent pebble which he called clogh-greena and kept under his hand on the table during the lesson. As a child in Hertfordshire I had found and treasured several of these pebbles which also were called sun-stones, so I already knew about them. They are, Brien told me, a powerful charm against the Gentry, yet another disguising name for fairies.

STAYING IN but looking out. A cruel, cold, black storm; ugly, sullen, treacherous, growling and snarling on the Strand, throttling the rocks.

Baby, who is nearly nineteen months old, has suddenly realized that he is a person. He is shy about it; looks in the glass and blushes, looks away, self-conscious and a little frightened. He hides his face in my neck and holds me fast for safety, and to assure himself that he is still a part of me, in spite of being suddenly himself, a small and helpless child.

He cried when Nanny put him in his cot, and for the first time wanted her to stay with him.

Poor darling little atom.

TO C.L.C. [a first cousin of Mary's mother] who is ill.

My darling C.,
Will not *anyone* write to tell me how you are? I feel certain you are better, for surely I should know if you are worse. I pray that you are free from pain. I know that you are in *Kewn Kreestha*, the lovely Irish for the Quiet of Christ. See, I write to you living and not dying, for why should you die who are still young and have so much to give? "There is sand in your glass yet and your sun is not gone down."

I am sending you wave after wave of my love and vitality so that you must get better; you are better; you are well enough to have an egg "to your tea".

A NIGHT OF STARS. Kneeling at my open window until my head inside goes round and round, dazed by the wonder and the glory of the heavens, and my frustrated mind takes refuge in the Psalms.

The sea gives an impression of far-off-ness and immensity, even though the horizon is but a few miles away. At night, sea and sky run together. I know of the horizon only when a star climbs out of the hidden water, or when the young moon is drowned.

At sunset, a chain of flat, dusky clouds passed like rafts across the red sky. I saw them an hour later, forlorn craft without a harbour, holding on to the moon.

I CAME HOME by the lake road this frosty, crimson evening and saw one and then another woodcock, flying low, making for the thin wood where they lodge.

They feed at night along the margin of the lake, sensing their prey by the nerves in their long beaks; on Kilkerran's strand one can see the holes made by their bills.

The "clean and tidy woodcock" washes in running water in the early morning after his night of feeding, before going back to his sleeping bush.

They leave us as suddenly as they come; for the moon, the country people say.

BABY was sitting on the hearthrug before the fire in his dressing-gown, "telling" his toes: "Harry Whistle, Tommy Thistle, Harry Whibble, Tommy Thibble, and little Oker Bell."

Then his fingers: "Tom Thumpkin, Ben Bumpkin, Bill Winkin, Long Linkin, and little Dick."

My fingers have other names: "Thumbkin, Foreman, Middleman, Ringman, Littleman." And Amy, the shy new nursery maid from Somerset, has yet another set; "Thumb, Toncher, Longman, Lecheman, Littleman."

Afterwards I look up "Lecheman" in the dictionary, and find that the apothecary (leach) of old used his third finger for tasting his medicines.

When I am quite uncertain in one of my minds, or one part of my mind, whether there be any heaven or any future existence, another mind or another part knows quite well that there is a heavenly stronghold and refuge, a safety in which most certainly my soul shall find harbourage.

This second mind is at peace and quietly amused at the doubts of the other mind. And then suddenly something happens. Some vast coiled body that stretches from east to west, wrapped in thick clouds, wakes and stirs. It coils and uncoils its monstrous shape and hisses, "There is nothing but nothingness for you, for all of you."

Both minds stagger and are lost in deep darkness; they run blindly to and fro, shrieking, because they are betrayed; until the mind that doubted lays hold of the other, screaming "Stop! We shall not know, we shall not know! Thank God for annihilation."

The good mind comes to itself. "Peace, peace," it cries, "the peace of God shall keep our minds through Jesus Christ."

ON A BLEAK, colourless day, I graft an imaginary interest or beauty on to some dull object. The sand-hills, dull in the sad light of a winter afternoon, turn into the desert round the Sphinx and Pyramids.

The silence is broken by the creaking of a shadow of lifting water from a ditch. I hear the muffled shuffling of camels' pads and see bare-necked vultures high in a cloudless sky. What matter if the creaking comes from the unoiled wheels of Mrs Michael Bridget Donovan's ass-cart and the birds of prey are Irish gulls?

Blake played at this game:

> With my inward eye 'tis an old Man grey;
> With my outward a Thistle across my way.

TODAY Jacky and I went out in a terrific gale against the advice of Carmody and Jenkins. We went by the south road which is sheltered first by woods and then, partially, by the sand-hills.

On the small space of road between sand-hills and cliffs occasional waves broke across, to the discomfiture of donkeys and their drivers returning from market. One or two of the men "had drink taken" and spoke their minds.

"G'wan now, ye bliddy little divil!" They used their blackthorns freely.

"Do you think that's how Balaam shouted to his donkey?" Jacky asked. "Do you think he called it a bliddy little divil? What is bliddy?"

We dashed across between two waves and fell breathless into the shelter of the little quarry a few yards beyond the road. The donkeys plunged through froth and foam to the noise of oaths, and sticks rattling on their ribs. Mrs Michael Bridget Donovan went last, shrieking invocations to Heaven.

"Howly Mother … howly …" A wave curdled round donkey and cart.

"Be all the Howlies ..." shrieked the terrified woman, dropping the rope reins and crossing herself vigorously. There was no real danger, and the gallant ass struggled out of the retiring waves encouraged by the yells and laughter of the merry men on the other side.

Poor frightened Bridget! She expects her seventh child in a week or two.

When we came out of the quarry into the open, the wind refused to let us climb higher but threw us against the gate in the wall which bounds Croachna. We fell through the gate and crouched on the inner side of the wall to regain breath.

Here among thick brambles were huddled scores of little birds, sheltering from the storm. They seemed dazed by the noise in the air and took no notice of us. We crept into Rahavarrig Wood and made our way home through densely growing stunted trees and laurels where woodcock were hiding.

I was thankful to reach the comparative quiet of the house and to hand Jacky over to his anxious Nanny. In the nursery; tea being laid, Baby in his high chair hammering on the table with a spoon. He looked at his storm-tossed mother and brother with a wide grin. At the nursery door I hear Jacky say:

"Nanny, the Battery men call a donkey a bliddy little divil. What does bliddy mean? Don't you know? Then you won't *do* anything to me if I call Baby a bliddy little divil, will you? A divil is a fallen angel, *Mum* says, but Mike Madden says it's anything from a policeman to a wurrum."

"Sit up to your tea," says Nanny sternly.

AT NIGHT, the great wind which I so much love, battering on walls and windows, is a friend whose turbulent passion I understand. But the mean little winds which sneak at night through window crevices, hiding under the swelling carpet and then without a sound clutching at my bare legs, are dreadful, hostile, like stoats grabbing a rabbit.

If only I could kick them off! I hurry with fluttering nightgown, and they at my heels, into the bed's safety.

Even then, unless I dive under the bedclothes, they fly at my throat.

We have a fine library but nothing later than 1840. I get books from London but I lack guidance in the choice of them and help to understand them. Jacky is constantly commenting on my ignorance and inability to answer his questions. (All the same I am not ignorant!) I have bought

Encyclopedia Britannica, and we search together for information. "Is it true, Mum, is it truer than Mike Madden?"

In my mind is desolation. I want to grow, to learn, to be taught. Here there are no teachers. I am as stunted as the trees on the edge of our wind-swept woods.

IT IS A COLD and frosty night after a sunny cold day. Jacky and I walked in the woods. Here and there the frost was still white; on fallen leaves we saw the little pricks of mice claws. Robins showed themselves, their way when they are hungry. We ruffled over a leaf-drift and exposed worms and slugs to which we left them. Jacky felt worried because we can't be kind to robins without being cruel to worms.

"Why didn't God make owls and robins to eat groundsel instead of mice and worms? Does groundsel feel when it is being gnawed by cater-pillars?"

I HAVE THROWN fifty pounds away. It was in an endeavour to drain and get rid of the rushes in the field near the west lodge. Duthie the steward said it could be done.

I am told too late that the old labourers laughed as they carried out his orders. " 'Twas there the sea come when Croachna was an island; 'twas there the last of the sea lay when the rest of it had drawn away to the west. 'Tis too low to drain."

So, there in the old sea bed, until the sea turns to its old channel, green will grow the rushes.

In this rushy field, at times, the early and late mists are born, low-lying, dank and blank, or huddled and lumpy, or quiet as hooded watchers of the dead; at other times, jostling wispily at the bidding of some low-creeping, furtive wind.

I have seen them at dawn dancing in quick, fantastic curves as the sun rises and sends them about their business.

I COULDN'T DO the flowers in the church in the morning on account of a headache so when I started out for my drive in the afternoon I arranged for my basket of flowers to be sent up to the church and for the key to be left in the door. On the way home I was dropped at the church path and walked up, feeling all in a dream from a high temperature and the Phenacetin which I had to take for the intense pain.

The church door was open and from within came a loud busy hum of voices. I went in, it was all like the happening of a dream, and found a mob of strange peasants, all men except one. I stood inside the door feeling very Protestant and outraged and a tiny bit frightened for they looked rather brigandish.

So, summoning my courage and dignity, I addressed the first who turned round and saw me. "What do you want in this church?" He was half drunk and lurched close up. "Nothin' particular then, Miss."

"I am Lady Carbery," I said shortly, and then they all turned and cringed, murmuring, "sure and 'twas no harrm they meant," so I forgave them and smiled upon them as they filed out. I left the door open and did the flowers, and after a bit they and others all came in again, all strangers, about 35 or 40 of them. I didn't feel quite happy, all alone with such a gang, so I faced them and said, "You are welcome to look round and to look at the monument of old Lord John"(whose name is a byword for goodness in West Cork) "and then you must go."

They stared at the organ and asked one another what it was. Only one or two had ever heard an organ (and they the great travellers!), so I thought why not play to them. So I seized a boy and showed him how to blow; he was *scared* at raising the wind like that, and I sat down and played. Their faces were delightful, surprise, astonishment, delight. I played whispering soft things so as not to frighten them, at first, and at last "The Wearin' of the Green", that lovely wistful song. They sighed with feeling and when I stopped they said "Thank you Ma'am", and shuffled away. I thought I had seen the last of them, but no, back came an old man; he must be a hundred I should think. This time I learned why they are here.

They had come to bury a woman in a family grave, come from miles and miles away in the West. They were too poor to pay a priest, so they opened the grave, took out two or three mouldering old coffins, laid her in, put back the old coffins and covered them all up, a foot or two of earth and that was enough. The eldest relation said a prayer.

It gave me a strange feeling, the thought of those old coffins coming up with the light and air, with the poor dead things inside who had been so long in the dark, for tho' I do not let myself think of the dead in any way bound within bodies, and no more than used garments of the spirit, now and then it comes over me that I want to talk to them and comfort them, to look over the familiar fields and tell them about the haymaking; my eyes to see for them, my ears to hear.

I WENT, in the delicious wind, on the car to Ross, with Baby and his Nanny holding on but delighted. I was carrying a rolled up and magnificent poster, which Jacky and I painted yesterday in red and black, to advertise the Industrial Exhibition to be held in Cork. We pasted the printed schedule of prizes below. The "Mayor of Ross" (Old Walsh the saddler and our staunch ally) nailed it on a board, hoisted it aloft in the market square and summoned the town crier!

Meanwhile I strolled in and out of the funny shandredaus, horse-carts, ass-carts, cyars and floats. From all sides came kindly greetings in sweet singing voices. Three little kids were offered to Baby. They were on their way to the butcher to make Easter lamb.

I lost the car in the crowd. It was hidden between a load of turf and a netted pig cart, and much amusement was caused. It tickled the people, the mere idea of the car being lost in so small a market place, and there were ejaculations on all sides: "Wirra! wirra! an' the cyar gone! Faix! Whativer will her poor ladyship do? It's Mike (Walsh) will carry her to the Castle! Meself then would bring her safe home."

As I drove away I heard the tinkle of the town crier's bell calling attention to the poster. I'm as fond of its red and black gaiety hanging on the market hall as an artist of being "on the line" at the Academy. Jacky ought to have come, but he does get so mobbed.

I DIDN'T get up till 10 today. The post brought letters from both Bats with further commands, which meant several letters for me to write. Then came word that Mr Hodges is still ill, and a message from Nell of the Battery, my first friend. A bare-legged boy brought the message, a little fellow who must "spake himself wid the ladyship". He couldn't trust six-feet-of-footman to tell me the truth.

"Well, Paddy, what is the matter?"

"'Tis me Gran'mother! 'Tis Nell that your ladyship know very well. She do be dyin'."

"Dying? Who says so?"

"The Docther, Miss, me Ladyship. He've been an' he can do nothin' more, an' last night Father anointed me Gran'mother. An' he will not be seein' her annymore."

"Is your mother with her?"

"She do be alone in the bed then. Me mother's at the fair an' me father at the fishin', an' the childer at school an' me Gran'mother do be wishful for the ladyship."

"Of course I'll come, Paddy. If you wait you can drive back with me."

While the cobs and Nobbs were getting ready, Paddy had some food. He is very thin and starved, with big blue eyes and a red button of a nose and a wide smiling mouth.

We went in the wagonette. Nobbs and Paddy sat behind, Paddy rolled in the "mourning" rug that Algy and I bought at Biarritz at "Old England" when we were mourning his father. (We mourned handsomely in those days. It was there that I made him black serge breeches to play golf in.) That black rug was honoured now by being kept for the purpose of rolling round passengers like Paddy. I should have liked him to sit beside me in the front but Nobbs would have been outraged. The air was very *douce* and the sun life-giving. I took deep breaths of air to fortify me against cabin-stuffiness.

When we got there, however, the cottage was fairly clean, in spite of the hens scratching about on the earth floor. Dear old Nell was heaped up on a bunk in a space three foot by two. The rest of the "bed" was occupied by a heap of coal. Quite clearly Nell was starving. "Look in me face," she whispered, "d'y'see, have I the death?" I looked critically at her, professionally, but also with affection, and I could see no shadow.

"Truthfully, Nell, you have not got the Death in your face. I think you will get well."

"Glory be to God and his blessed Mother, an' me anointed an' ready."

"Tell me, Nell, when did you last have food?"

"Food, is it? An' what'd a dyin' woman want wid food an' the children hungry? 'Twas yesterday, then, a sup o' tay ..."

"You shall have soup, hot soup in a minute. Lie still while I heat it."

I had the soup with me in a wine bottle, but the puzzle was how to heat it. Not a saucepan could I find. There was nothing but the bastable and the great kettle full of cold water.

Paddy was nowhere to be seen. He had probably disappeared with Nobbs who was keeping the cobs from catching cold. A five-year-old child appeared from a dark corner, sucking its finger and looking shyly at me from among its uncombed locks. "Can you find me anything to make the soup hot?" I asked it very gently. It doesn't do to startle these *leprechauns*.

It sidled about the cabin and produced a cracked teapot, and at the same moment I saw an old tin on a shelf which held a few grains of tea. I shook the tea out and poured soup in and set it in the hot embers on the hearth. The child put all its weight on the bellows handle and blew, puffing out its thin cheeks and proud to be helping the lady.

While the soup was heating I moved the coal, the large bits which could be handled, and smoothed down the slack as best I could so that Nell could stretch out her cramped legs. She had a sack under her filled with wheat husks gathered at our last threshing, over her she had the ghost of a blanket, a sheet black with age and her own cloak. Under her head was a ticking filled with straw.

I helped her to drink some water, and when the soup was warm, fed her from a large mussel shell which I picked up outside in the road. It was a lovely blue shell lined with silver and opal, fit for a queen.

The leprechaun looked reproachfully at me and, after some desultory examination of the floor, produced a filthy old spoon. Nell swallowed the soup and asked for more so the tin refilled went back into the embers and the leprechaun blew the bellows once and then went out at the door to chase away a pig that must have smelt soup.

Nell looked at me searchingly and whispered: "The priest said … an' the docther said … an' me darter an' me son said the same …"

"Any of us may be mistaken, Nell," I told her. "I may be mistaken, but I think you have several years of life before you! I do really!"

"An' so do I think," she answered, stretching first one leg and then the other, making the small coal trickle off the bunk on to the floor. "An' wid the help av God an' your ladyship, 'tis back to me own little house I'll be goin', an' not be livin' wid them that would let me die wid years av life yet in me! If your ladyship would tell the steward to have the hole in the roof mended an' a load av firin' sent down, it's on the bare floor av me own houseen I'll be goin'! For 'tis better to be alone in me house wid God than wid them that'd wish ye in the grave."

Here she had a few more shells of our beautiful strong consommé. Every minute she grew stronger. "I dunno what'll Father say, an' me anointed an' all! An' me darter! Me darter did be sayin' that she'd find me dead when she'd be back from the fair," Nell chuckled.

"Well, anyhow, Nell, I hope she won't have ordered your coffin."

At this she laughed outright. "'Twas your ladyship was to bring the coffin, but mebbe me darter'll bring the whiskey for the wake!"

I came away with some misgivings. I must go again tomorrow to see about getting the old dear back to her own house.

I FELT very small yesterday but amused. I had to go to Ardfield Girls School to make a list of the girl exhibitors' names. I was worried by the way they spelt their names, with their ahs and their hahs and their aws. I wrote one name at a guess as Flanahan! Later I showed it to the teacher who smiled and said most politely, "It is quite right, your ladyship, and it will do quite well. It is only that we do just sometimes spell it Flavin!"

Could good manners go further? How utterly un-Saxon they are! How brutally downright we must seem to the sensitive Celt.

Yesterday, I had just stepped into the brougham at the door and the footman was hurriedly scrambling on to the box, when I spied a ragged Tim standing by. My good Angel told me, "This is Cornelius."

"I think I know you! You are Cornelius O'Leary?"

"You know me very well, my Ladyship. I am C O R R N A Y L I U S."

MRS DOUGLAS is so happy at the West Lodge and her weird little daughter who appears to believe that she is in fairyland. She was born partly paralysed, blind and with a cataract. One eye was operated on a few years ago so she sees a very little. A pitiful but wonderfully happy little creature, helpless, dwarfed in body, sweet and loving in heart. She sits on the fringe of the wood all day long listening to the larks in the meadows and on the hills.

Her name is Dimple and she makes up fairy stories. When I called this evening her mother told me that Dimple had made up a story about a fairy princess called Lady Carbery, who lent poor children and their mothers fairy houses in fairy land; and who would one day appear from the wood, walking between the ferns, and would speak to her.

Thro' the wood I came at twilight and stopped by her chair. How good of my Guardian Angel to bring me that way. "Are you Lady Carbery?" she asked, peering at me with her strange blue eyes and putting out a warm soft little hand. "Are you a fairy princess?"

"We are all that sort here," I told her, "and now you are one of us. We are all fairy landers and very happy."

She clapped her hands and laughed like a silver bell.

AS I WAS WALKING OUT this afternoon we passed a little house and a child came flying out through the door with, hard on its heels, a hen hurtling thro' the air upside down, evidently thrown. I looked inside and there in the house were six children having a battle in the absence of their mother. They were all crying at once.

"Stop!" I said, and they stopped.

"Now, comfort one another at once!" I ordered them.

"We will, Miss. Is it Lady Carbery, Miss?"

Next a woman came up whose "inthide" is badly hurt. She is Katty Donovan, the mother of the supposed fairy child whom I saved from being roasted for a changeling. The fairy has now become a "faire stout choild". She hailed me. "I've been waitin' to ask what'll I do about my 'inthide'?" She should have gone to Cork two months ago, but is finally going next week.

A nice creature. The priest made her marry a linen-draper's assistant from Clonakilty whom she didn't care for at all and why should she, "and him shtuck down in a town and no use at all on the little farm. Whativer tuk the priest at all?"

Lastly to the house, my destination (and the soup's) where the sick child was dragged out of bed and flopped down on the earth floor where it sat drooping like a little flower, seven years old and dying. She won't eat a morsel …

I HAD a crowded journey by the mail on Friday night and was glad of a bath and breakfast at Euston. Then fittings. My new stays, 20 inch, which means my waist is 21 again outside my dress, glory be! At Jays I suddenly fainted and found myself among the pins on the floor, the fitters fanning me and holding smelling salts to my excruciated nose.

At the Pré. Rather depressing here. Evelyn, thin, haggard, dressed in muslin and sash and baby hat as if she were sixteen, feverishly excited over the terrific rubbish that is arriving as wedding presents. In the intervals of unpacking she sentimentally wonders how she can bring herself to leave her happy home where every blade of grass is dear to her.

Hitherto no words have been strong enough to express her hatred of it and us. The future is dark, for we know she will detest being poor and I tremble to think of the life she will lead the poor man. He seems to have an idea that they will both be here whenever they choose, and Mother is so good, she will find it hard to nip his fond hopes in the bud.

The Best Man has arrived. He is no Vere de Vere. We shall all be glad when the wedding is over. About 120 people are coming so let us hope for a fine day.

Evie, altho' she looked quite ghastly-pale, enjoyed her wedding immensely. It went off very well and I saw many old friends, people came from a distance all round. Her wedding dress was lovely. We all looked charming, especially Mabel in pink, and dear little Con in her bridesmaid's white frock and a wreath of roses in her dark hair.

Mother is most glad to have Evie off her hands and whatever we feel now and may feel in the future about *Him*, we must look upon him as a Universal Benefactor and be kind in consequence. I think he is genuinely fond of her.

I am doing all I can to help Evie, but it is difficult and one cannot do anything *con amore*. It is the tragic truth that not one soul, rich or poor, laments her departure, not one will miss her. How very sad that is.

1 PORTMAN SQUARE

It is snowing this afternoon, a cutting icy wind. I came in frozen and very tired to find no fire in my room, windows and doors open, snow on the carpet. I took the housemaid with the house and she is a demon. Tepid water, tepid hot water tray, tepid early tea! Take it or leave it! Well, I will lay upon her a proper Irish curse!

I met a physiognomist at a tea party today who approved highly of my virtuous physiognomy. It appears that, unknown to me, I have *moral ears*.

I should think with moral ears I could safely take a walk after 6 p.m. whatever Cousin Cassie says. If accosted I shall say: "See the answer in my ears." I shall think a lot more of my ears in future. Hitherto I have only acknowledged their beauty. How fortunate to be both beautiful and moral.

I also met an evangelical at the same party. He had a nasty eye and moist hands with a furtive squeeze in them. He had a nerve, to claim to explain the Lord's intentions with regard to my soul. A brazen serpent.

After him I met a bitter creature who thinks women should have votes. "I'm sorry, I don't want a vote," I said politely. "You wouldn't," she replied bitterly. "You're too pretty."

What a snub! But I don't care! I have moral ears to hold me up in the face of mine enemies.

TODAY I shopped in my sables. Such an advantage! One gets the attention of the great ones of the earth, such as Mr Hiley at Jays; also unlimited credit should one wish it. My sables got me a perpetual permit to examine the most secret and precious manuscripts at the British Museum at my will. A fur coat is heavy to carry on one's back but worth the weight.

MYSELF, John and Ralfe are to be painted by Mr Shannon. The sittings begin tomorrow, all three of us to be in white. I have had a frock made on purpose of soft satin.

The sitting. The studio is terribly cold for my thin frock and bare neck. I find it exhausting. Ralfe is naughty and won't stand up, slides down and I have all his weight to bear on my arm. John says sittings are beastly fag. He worries poor Mr Shannon by keeping count of the cigarettes he smokes. We are now on canvas in white paint, like clowns but with brown hair.

I TOOK my Bible and inned wi' me finger, and lighted on: "Paul thanked God and took courage." I do need courage and a stronger will.

I came upon another wise motto in a book, *Advice to Women Who Wish for a Tranquil Life, By a Woman* ... "Eat in company but sleep alone." Cousin Cassie believes in that advice for people like her and me who appreciate the friendship and company by day of men. She has her delightful padres to talk and listen to but I have no one in the *desart vast* of my home.

THE XMAS CURSE is weighing me down and I dash frenziedly from shop to shop with my present list that seems to well up like the oil in the widow's cruse and never to be done. I do give "gold" where I can, and if only the rest would be content with frankincense and myrrh, I shouldn't be so near a breakdown. I dream of dress-lengths, umbrellas, gloves, scarves, stockings, toys, books, chocolates and crackers, and the hundred fancy gifts needed for friends, and the Castle Freke children.

Let no one give me anything! The whole system is wrong, and reduces women to raving lunatics. There was none of it when I was a child and no one had presents but the servants and the poor. Xmas meant a length of dress stuff for each maid, cashmere or merino for the uppers, a neat print for the unders, a tie for the men or warm socks. Beef for the garden and farm people, crossovers made by ourselves for our pet old women.

We children had no presents except on birthdays. Why should we? "It is more blessed to give than to receive." We knew that must be true because it was in the Bible but we found it a difficult precept and poor compensation for our empty stockings on Xmas morning. Now present giving is a millstone round one's neck, the labour, the thinking, remembering, hunting, buying and packing up the endless letters. People I love best I keep to last. If I break before Xmas under the strain, they will understand and forgive, if there is anything to forgive. There is only one thing worse than this Xmas present giving, and that is present getting.

THE PICTURE has been sketched in today. Sitting is a tiring business because it involves keeping both boys good and amused.

Shannon is a dear, Irish American. He said to me: "I felt sure you are Irish the first time I saw you!" Me! Irish! Yes, me! Was I pleased?

IN LONDON, I saw the Queen today in the Park. There was such a pack of carriages, glorious horses, some cruelly reined up with bearing reins, others shabby-genteel, hanging their heads, and a few come up from the suburbs, shaggy, unclipped, hot and moist. Behind them funny ramshackle shays driven by whiskered men in bowler hats, they and their fares agog and aglow with loyalty. I felt quite loyal too and full of admiration and affection for the Little Old Lady.

I AM SPENDING long hours at the British Museum working on Mrs Elizabeth Freke's Diary. Today, being tired and needing a change of subject, I got hold of a small book in Greek and German of the poems of Crete.

I made a few translations, poor enough:

> Leave thou me not when comes the hour to part;
> Kiss thou my eyes which have the light forgot;
> Bind thou my cold dead hands upon my heart
> And stay awhile. My sweet, forsake me not.
>
> Before the face of Love all fear takes wing,
> Thro' flames of fire she goes nor heeds their sting;
> Deep waters cannot drown, nor storms dismay,
> And singing she pursues her radiant way.

A DREADABLE DAY. I have to go to a luncheon party. I shall find half a dozen women gathered together, most alarming. Collectively they frighten me with their hard eyes, individually I usually can get behind their masks and see into their hearts, more or less. Men, except fox-hunters and guardsmen, I find much easier.

Oh me! I would rather be going out to lunch with a party of nice dogs or a wise old parrot. I do not wish to be inside the Squirrel Cage of society, turning round and round, luncheons, teas, dinners, bridge, plays, twiddle, twaddle, day after day. I want to be in the interesting Ruskin, Matthew Arnold set, only I don't know how to get in. I can't go to University College and knock and say to the secretary, "Please introduce me to your professors", or to the B.M. heads of departments and say "Let me in to your friendship." I have no scientific friend except my dear Sir David Gill, who is out of England.

BACK at Castle Freke. Chapel Mary lives alone in her cabin on the road above Milltown. She is the caretaker of the Roman Catholic church. In her spare time she knits, attends to her pig and her hens, and collogues, rather coarsely, with the neighbours who pass her door. She is a jovial creature who might have stepped out of a Rowlandson drawing.

When I called on her today, however, I found her sitting beside the fire, her hair rough, her eyes red, her big square feet nervously shuffling on the earth floor. Her hands were pleating and unpleating her apron. A thin little cat twined about her legs. I sat down and waited.

"The last time ye sat in that chair, me lady, a couple o' months ago, wasn't I knittin' stockin's for me son in Americky?" said Chapel Mary. "Ye'll remember the snail pattern, goin' round and round the leg?"

"I remember. A difficult pattern!"

"It was so. And this marnin' ..."

There was a long silence while she struggled with her tears, brushing them away with an angry hand.

"This marnin' I come down the stairs from the loft. I was thinkin' 'twas a fine day for farmers, for the sun was shining in by the windy, an' shinin' on me table. On him that was lyin' the length of the table ..."

She covered her face with her hands and wept aloud.

"It was me son who lay there, an' him dead," she cried in a loud high voice. "Someone had dressed him in his dark clothes, an' on his legs the stockin's I knitted for him in the snail pattern. I tell ye, me lady, I saw me boy as clear as I see ye! His hands be his sides, his eyes not so shut but he seemed to see his mammy lookin' down on him. Och, God help me ..."

She rocked to and fro as she wept. I tried to comfort her by reminding her that her son had not really been lying on the table.

"Me son is dead," she said hopelessly. "I left him lyin' there while I hurried to Mrs Duggan, to bring her to see him. When we got to the door he was gone. The table was there just the same, wid the sun still searchin' it but himself was gone from me. Jasus and Mary help him."

I sat with her until neighbours arrived to hear the strange news, then I came away, bewildered.

Mrs Duggan believes in these warnings. When she was a little girl of seven years, she and a five-year-old brother were playing beside Kilkerran Lake. There were reapers working in the field beside them, but the little fella fell into deep water. The weeds held him and hid him. He was drowned before anyone knew.

The little girl was sent to tell her mother, who at that time lived in the keeper's cottage. Her mother stood in the doorway with a white face. "Ye need not tell me," she cried, "haven't I seen him? He came to me, he was here with me, wet, with the green weed clingin' to him, the water runnin' over him. He is drowned."

I ADD this note two weeks later. Mrs Duggan has been to tell me that a letter came this morning for Chapel Mary. It was from America. Mary took it in her hand to the Rectory for Mr Hodges to read it, as she is not herself a scholar.

"His Riverance took it and give a quick look. 'Sit down, me poor woman,' he said to her, 'for bad news is in the letter,' and he put a chair under her where she stood, tremblin'.

"'Poor Dan,' he read, 'is dead. It was sudden in the end; 'twas an impression on the chest and the heart failin' him.'"

"The letter," Mrs Duggan explained, "was from the woman where he lodged, an Ardfield woman, and there would be many Castle Freke people in the same place.

"They waked him from night to mornin', his friends and neighbours round him. He made a handsome corpse, death became him well. Herself had put on him his best clothes; she put the new stockin's on him that his mother sent him for Christmas, them in the snail pattern."

"How is Mary?"

"She's quiet. She has no more tears. She has them all shed in the past two weeks. She is busyin' herself about the wake, God help her."

A[RTHUR] S[ANDFORD] has sent me notepaper stamped "Paradise", in honour of the Paradise in the shrubbery where Doty and her mother planted narcissi and did Sunday lessons; which I discovered grown over and had cleared. Its name was also carved last Sunday on a tree by A.S.

While he was carving I thought I would go for a solitary walk, leaving him to it, but he said if I did he would spell Paradise with a 'c' and there it would be for ever.

He seems nervous of being alone in that haunted shrubbery; but that is only a ruse to keep me there.

The children have colds and are not to come downstairs.

When I go to see them in their warm nursery, Jacky is busy dissecting an engine and doesn't want to be disturbed. Baby is being rubbed with embrocation before the fire.

I slip into a fur coat and go out. What a glory meets me!

> Sharp is the night, but stars with frost alive
> Leap off the rim of earth across the dome,
> It is a night to make the heavens our home.

The grass is crunchy with white frost. The leafless trees bud and blossom with stars. Star-sparks lie in the rimey mouths of the old cannons, rime is on the terrace wall and on the tiny spears of moss in its crevices.

The sea is a soft shadow between earth and blazing sky.

FATHER O'BRIEN came to luncheon. He turns up once a week. It makes a break in the week for the good old man.

He loves to tell of his young days at Louvain, where he was trained, and to air a few French words; a simple peasant with a feudal loyalty and affection for "the family".

I told him I had had a deputation of his women parishioners, begging me to ask him to preach shorter sermons. "They have to sit on the floor of the church; the stones are cold and damp, they say. What do you think, Father? Could you be shorter?"

"I could not," he answered. "My God gives me a message to deliver to the people. Let the stones be cold and damp, I can't help it, that willn't stop me. I begin, and I go on, till I get to the end of the message."

We talked of the hard lot of labourers who work for small farmers; they get a day's work every now and then for miserable pay, less than a shilling for ten or twelve hours; also of the wretchedness of tenants whose landlords are men of their own class. Neither farmers nor many of this sort of landlord show consideration or pity for poverty.

"The peasant doesn't complain; he has a poor opinion of himself," Father O'Brien said. "He makes no attempt to improve in any way. He's been trodden under foot for centuries and knows he is of no account. When persons like yourself wish to help him, maybe to give him decent clothes, he thinks it queer, unnatural. Why should 'the quality' trouble about the likes of him, he thinks."

There are, of course, exceptions, but I have noticed that when a person in this country does something that is in the least altruistic, people of a slightly more educated class imagine one must have an axe to grind. They look for a selfish motive. Axe-grinders themselves, they cannot believe in simple kindness, in the wish to serve.

When I take patients to the hospitals, these axe-grinders whisper, " 'Tis to plaze the docthers. Not everyone would trust himself to them *hospitables*, where they chop the leg off you as aisy as look at you, or whip the eye out of your head between one wink and another ... where there's nusses who strip you and lay you in the bath without shame, nor caring if ye die on the spot from wetting the whole of you."

When at last they come to see that I have no axe, *ever*, to grind, they shrug their shoulders, thinking me a bit quare in the head.

CHRISTMAS EVE. Bellemère, who is staying, asked a lot of questions about A.S., whether he is fast? Does he gamble, smoke immoderately, drink, run into debt, swear? Is he a Christian?

At bedtime I went with their mother to see the visitor children asleep and to put presents beside their beds. Then I slipped into the night-nursery and looked at Baby, who opened his eyes and smiled at me. Nanny's merino stocking, bulging with promise, hung from the cot's knob.

The night is mild. The velvety darkness is pricked with tiny lights. Tonight, Christmas candles are burning in the windows of every house and cabin over all the land. Every door is on the latch. The poorest peasant lights a candle to guide the Infant Jesus to the warmth and welcome of his home.

It is 3 a.m. and I cannot sleep. I have been thinking of all the "Mary" legends I know, and hearing in imagination the lark's song, a gold and silver cascade on the darkness.

> Ever 'gainst that season comes,
> Wherein our Saviour's birth is celebrated,
> The bird of dawning singeth all night long:
> So hallow'd and so gracious is the time.

Christmas Day. I have had four very precious presents from exceedingly poor people. One is a book-marker made of an ancient ribbon, possibly from the dress of "Lady Catherine" of sixty years ago, washed and pressed and threadbare; a matchbox covered with shells, from a sick child; an old Christmas card carefully backed with pink blotting-paper; and a small bronze pincushion made from a baby's shoe. Immense time, care and ingenuity have gone to their making.

Jacky hurried into my bed at 9. "Oh look!" It was the huge magnet A.S. had sent him. Such joy, and one present after another, many too many.

The carol singers came at 12.15; a sweet chiming of old voices, to be exact more like a sawing of wood. A soft delicious gale has been blowing all morning, my sort of weather.

Baby "saw" A.S. again in my brooch this evening. It was curious. "He's doing something about Mum's finger." "But is Mum there?" "No, but he is doing something about Mum's finger." (A.S. sent me a thimble for an Xmas present. Rather late!)

BELLEMÈRE talked again about A.S. Anxious I should marry him, but thinks I don't like him well enough. She is very practical and full of plans and certainly "premature".

Xmas is sad. Bellemère does not see the empty chairs as I do.

I have a sore throat. I stayed in and cried in private brown tears. Tears should be blue and luminous and round and smooth. Bellemère sat and talked at bed time. She thinks John is too much for me, needs a man's hand. She does dash ahead so. I feel like a drowning person.

"IN ITALY, Jacky, January 30th, 31st, and February 1st are called *giorni della merla*, days of the blackbird. Once, they say, the ancestor of all blackbirds was white. For these three days, always very cold, he had to take refuge in a chimney, which being sooty, made him black, so that his descendants have been black ever since.

"In Scotland and parts of Ireland he is called merle. Shakespeare called him

> the ouzel cock so black of hue
> with orange tawny bill."

"Thank you, Mum, I don't want to hear any more about merles. I haven't got any more patience. Tell me a story."

"Once upon a time, there was a saint, a very good Irishman, called Kevin. He used to say his prayers in a church at Glendalough.

"He stretched out his joined hands when he prayed. One day a hen-blackbird laid eggs on the palms of his outstretched hands. 'Och, the poor merle,' he said, looking down on the eggs, 'sure, 'twill never do to disappoint her, and her with great faith in her heart.' So he stayed where he was and didn't move until the little merles were hatched."

"Very silly," said Jacky, "and not true. I've heard something 'stronary about thrushes. When they are beginning to get old, they throw away their legs and grow new ones, but I don't believe that either."

"And in England people say toads sit on wheatear's eggs till they hatch."

"That can't be true; a toad has cold blood like a fish, or hasn't it?"

"I don't know. Yes, I do. It has warm blood. Anyhow, that story isn't true."

"Mike Madden says a wren's true name is Sally Droleen. On Christmas afternoon he and all the boys hunt Sally Droleen. They kill as many wrens as they can with sticks and stones, and next day the wren-boys bring the bodies round to get money. I told him it was debominable and if they hunt our wrens we shall have them sent to prison. Mike Madden said it has to be done, it always had been done and it's a religion, so they must. If no one ever gave the wren-boys money, wouldn't they stop it?"

"I'm sure they would, after a time."

"Anyhow, we won't give them a farthing. Mike Madden says the wagtail you're so fond of is the devil's bird and it's very dangerous to like it. If you say its name, Develing, you must only whisper it."

"Mike Madden talks a lot of nonsense."

"He's very intrusting. You know what we call a missel-thrush? Well, he and James McCarthy and Johnny Sweeney were arguing about its name. Mike called it a big felt, James said it was a butcher-bird and Johnny said it was a jay.

"I said, 'I'll tell you, it's a missel-thrush, I know it by its spots!' I asked Jenkins; he was coming up to do the flowers. 'That's a storm-cock,' Jenkins said, 'because it sings in storms.' Duthie came up and he said, where he came from, it was called Corney-Keevor. Wasn't it very worrying? Why should a plain bird have so many names?"

"I could tell you a few more; Screech, because of the way it shrieks when it's frightened."

"And Mathilde says, in France it's good to eat because it eats mistletoe berries, and it's called Grive and it can speak seven languages ... Oh, Mum, aren't we having a dreadfully untrue talk? I think we'd better stop."

The Irish call the dipper and common tern *kingfisher*; the hedge-sparrow is *black wren*; the fieldfare is *felty fare*, *big felt* or *blue felt*; the chiffchaff, sedge-warbler and willow-warbler are all *sally-pickers*; willow-warbler is also *golden wren*; the chough is *sea-crow*; and the tree-creeper is *woodpecker* or *tomtit*.

They know few bird names. More often "'tis 'a sart av a burd", or "a birdeen"!

THE WINTER is hard for the fishermen. There is sadness all round; so much poverty and distress.

One poor woman came today to show me two summonses for overdue rent and taxes. She would be "put out" tomorrow. I have lent her the money. She will pay me back in fish, lobsters and prayers! She went away rejoicing.

I should hate to be "put out" of my home. I often have to lend the people small sums to tide them over an emergency. If I'm not careful I shall turn into a "gombeen-man". Some come for clothes or because they are hungry, or for medicine.

Old Jerry Spillane who has been suffering from "a shtich in the shtomach and a great blow up", is cured, he says, by a "bottle" I gave him. It was milk powder. "Grand it was, it has given me *courage*, thanks be to God and your ladyship." One woman came for a bottle of "me Lady Carbery-ship's eye-water".

I can do so little for them and their gratitude is out of all proportion. I must be richer for their blessings! One woman told me that I am "as good as a Catholic for the poor".

As for me, I live out of doors, riding, walking, driving the five horses, 2 and 2 and 1.

MY ROOM is full of the scent of violets. A great bowl of them beside me, as I write, giving of their fragrance with all their might, and they the cheerful givers. They are so large and splendid that I feel a sudden wish they were small and lowly.

The sunsets yesterday and tonight have been glorious, over a calm turquoise sea. But how sad it makes me to look at this beautifulness alone. The reflection of their gold and purple in my heart is lost.

HEDGEHOG DAY. On this day, February 2nd, hedgehogs wake up and come out to see what the weather is like. Sometimes they stay awake; but if more cold weather is yet to come, they go to sleep again.

An hour ago, above Milltown, I heard the fussy warning of hens and ducks and the braying of the "little Irish Jacks". Miss Galway's rooks were wheeling wildly over her rookery; gulls were flying inland, diving in as though some enemy was after them. A storm brewing.

As I came back, blackbirds were singing shrilly in the shrubbery. Over the brow of Croachna, the little mountain sheep are filing down, picking their steps, making for the shelter of the trees under the hill.

ASH WEDNESDAY. The world was white when Kitty and I went out this early morning. Every bush and blade of grass was covered with hoar frost. Kitty thought it all very uncanny and shied vigorously from side to side.

We were taking things for Katty's fairy baby, who has a cold. On the way we met the whole community going to church, their foreheads newly washed in honour of the Ashes. Such kindly greetings they gave me, such friendly smiles.

JUST AS I AM by nature restless, a mover-on, so do I want to grow, and mentally to progress; to have a wider horizon, to "cross the ranges"; glad to be beyond, glad to change; not wishing to return on my tracks; leaving by the wayside the outworn things which have served their purpose; dropping impedimenta; to go on in the company of those of like mind; to part from those who, like Lot's wife, look back with regret. I want to go from strength to strength, "*im Ganzen, Guten, Wahren, resolut zu leben*".

I wrote that many years ago. In reality, in spite of my intention, because my will has not been strong enough and because my heart has governed my head; because for too long I was bound by ignorance, prejudice, convention, by mistaken ideals, by too rigid a sense of duty, by a too-rigid cleaving to the stern religious teaching of my youth; by circumstance, by my love of comfort, I have progressed but a short way.

I have not lived *im Ganzen*, no, not *im Halben*.

I am like one who tries to run a race weighed down by heavy clothing, by possessions, by the clinging of dear ones who hold them back. One who does not know the course, nor the nature of the obstacles nor the distance to be run, nor even the goal. But who, after long delay and much stumbling, noticing at last that other runners are in better trim, begins to cast away his burdens, lightens himself of heavy clothing and money, holds up his head and sees, though dimly, his goal.

What matter if I come in last and late in the day? What matter if I fall in the last lap? So long as I am running in the right direction when I fall.

Credo

I believe in God's Presence in all places, at all times.
He is among the primroses under the young and tender
    beech leaves,
He is beside the unfledged nestlings in their nests,
He plays with the children and their angels,
And is with the reapers in the cornfield.

On the lone hillside He watches while the shepherd sleeps,
While the sheep and lambs sleep in the darkness.
He bids the weary watchdog shut his eyes until the morning.

He walks beside the cripple on a stony road; the stumbling
    crutches are upheld by Him.
To the sick He brings dreams of health and walking in woods
    and meadows.
For the weak and restless He turns their pillows.

He gives to the ugly and deformed His compensation;
His visions for the blind, and for the deaf,
Songs in the night and chiming bells.

He watches beside all creatures trapped and caged,
And lepers, crying with blind eyes for their lost hands,
And outcast men and dogs, forsaken, spurned,
And Magdalene, in the anguish of her soul.

He is in prison with the criminal, in the despair and loneliness
    of his last night on earth;
In the trembling and fainting of his soul at daybreak;
And when they come for him, brotherly, with quick hands
    to bind him,
God gives him strength to climb the scaffold.

EPILOGUE:
THE CARBERY FAMILY
AFTER 1901

MANY YEARS later, Mary Carbery came to spend the last decade of her life in a cottage in the grounds of my father's home, Eye Manor, near Leominster in Herefordshire, England. She had married Arthur Sandford in 1901 and my father, Christopher, was their eldest son.

It was at Eye Manor, some time after Grandmother's death, that I discovered her journal when leafing through the drawers of a large mahogany wardrobe in the attic. Some of her possessions still lodged here: writing equipment, correspondence, drafts of letters and books, and the typescript of this journal – four volumes, bound in yellow covers secured with slightly rusty brass paper-clips, and entitled "From the Back of Beyond".

In the remaining pages of this book I will add some notes on what later became of Mary, and John and Ralfe, and Castle Freke, and her other children, and of her dreams and aspirations for them all.

WHEN Mary's first husband Algy realized that his pulmonary tuberculosis had left him little time to live, he and Mary departed on their last trip to the Malvern Hills in England, where they believed that the drier climate might allow him a few more weeks of life. Arthur Sandford, also known as "Kit", helped him on the start of this final journey by carrying the dying Lord Carbery on to the boat at Cork. Algy asked Kit to look after Mary when he was gone.

After three years had passed Kit decided he would like to marry Mary, but she was still not sure whether she wished to become closer to him. She writes, "You couldn't *possibly* be happy permanently yoked to a *Rebel*, an untamed and untamable Rebel ... a wild thing that might nestle momentarily at your fireside, even confidingly, so long as you held your breath and didn't speak or move." At the first conventional word or movement, she warned him, she "would start up and flee, away and away to the Heart of the Wilderness, where it would be *no use* your coming in search".

Kit was born in Kilvernon Rectory, County Tipperary, in 1859, the son of the Reverend William Sandford, Rector of Clonmel and Chancellor of Lismore Cathedral. His grandfather, Beech Sandford, was Archbishop of Clonmel, and his great grandfather, John Sandford, was "Monarch of Tuam". These Sandfords looked back to the medieval Bishop Sandford of Dublin and the Sandfords of Askham in Cumbria for their ancestry.

Kit was educated at Dr Knight's School, Camden Place, Cork, and studied medicine at Queen's College, Cork. By the time Mary met him, he had become the Consulting Surgeon at Cork Eye, Ear and Throat Hospital, of which he was a founder; Lecturer and Professor in Ophthalmology and Otolaryngology at University College, Cork; and a Member of the Board of Examiners for medical degrees at the National University of Ireland and Queen's University, Belfast.

Mary's sister Constance claimed that Arthur was nicknamed Kit because he resembled St Christopher, who is often pictured carrying the weak and vulnerable over rivers and fords. "The people of Cork had their own name for him," Constance wrote. "They called him 'God's Doctor' and loved him for his skill and great kindness."

The development of Mary and Kit's feelings for each other is chronicled in a series of letters between them, in one of which she recalls the first time he came to Castle Freke. As he walked "that long walk from the door to the fireplace end of the saloon", she remembered that it was Friday, and Good Friday at that, and that they had no fish. She was "quite reassured" when he "cheerfuly said yes to our excellent pressed beef".

After lunch Mary drove him in a donkey cart down to the beach and they walked over the cliffs. They stopped at the top to get their breath and Kit "shuddered and buttoned up his coat and complained of the East Wind". Then he "set to digging with great energy and cleverness by questions and severe eye probing".

As the relationship – which had been foreseen by Algy and given his blessing – grew deeper, Mary began to receive advice from her friends. Doty Bandon wrote that she had "prayed that you may be guided to do what is best". If Mary felt she could be "contented and happy" with Kit, then Doty was in favour. Another friend told her, "He is by a long way the best-looking man in Cork, tall, straight, strong, broad-shouldered but well proportioned, flat-backed!" Mary herself was experiencing feelings that she found confusing: "God made us a trinity, body, mind and spirit," she wrote. "The body not to be slighted or despised or treated as if it was the devil's contribution. I am afraid I have had always the puritanical idea of the body as a thing to be hard-worked and disregarded. All the same I am most thankful to God for letting me be tall and slim and pretty."

Kit had more to offer besides being the "best-looking man in Cork". Mary was both romantic and practical; but Kit was probably better at relating to other people, and was able to give reality to her dreams. He was adept at sorting out travel arrangements. He found dogs for the children, and a fine mare, Kitty, for Mary. Kitty's owner, he claimed, did not particularly need her, but, Mary says, "Of course, as I suspected at the time and verified soon after, Kitty had belonged to Kit himself and he was letting me have her." As a result she was not well received by Driscoll, his coachman, when she next visited his stables in St Patrick's Place in Cork.

"The master made a great mistake the day he let Kitty go," he said. "She was very sweet-tempered in the stables."

Mary ventured to say, humbly, "I do appreciate her very much. She has a good home."

"It was a good home she had here," he answered bitterly, "an' I liked her best of all the horses." Mary felt "withered".

A simpler person than Mary, Kit was less volatile and more dependable. He adored Mary and for her later gave up much of his career. As well as loving him Mary was to a degree in love with herself and probably loved him partly for the love of her she saw in him. She also valued him as a steadying influence on John and Ralfe, who had been showing signs of getting out of hand since their father's death. The earliest existing letter from John Carbery thanks Kit for a dog he had given him.

In 1902 Mary and Kit were married in the little church of All Saints in a pine wood at Branksome near Bournemouth, by Kit's elder brother Philip, who was vicar there.

After their wedding Mary and Kit lived at Castle Freke, and also spent time at his homes, No. 13 St Patrick's Place in Cork and Frankfield House near Cork. Kit possessed one of the first motor cars in Ireland, and rode or drove to work most mornings when he was not abroad. Mary and Kit had two sons, Christopher and Anthony.

No. 13 St Patrick's Place, now known as 12A, is a three-storey house whose ground floor is still used as a surgery and waiting-room. It occupies a corner site on the side of the steep St Patrick's Hill and had fine views, now partly obscured, over the city. Kit bought it in the 1880s. It is approached up steps from the street, leading to a classical portico. The stables and large garden, known to Mary and Kit as "Himmel Garten", that were at its back have now been replaced by another house.

Frankfield House, Kit's country residence in Douglas, a few miles from town, was in those days a small classical country house with farmland attached. In the woods behind it Mary and Kit created a garden. Frankfield is now a golf club and its greatest glory – past a romantic Monterey pine tree – consists of an extraordinary view of the city of Cork stretched beneath it.

Kit's duties kept him in Cork longer than suited Mary, and the pressures she put on him to forsake his career and concentrate on being her consort are already apparent in a letter of 1906, from Castle Freke, in which she describes loneliness as "the most dreadful thing in the world ... for all my roses, and my wood fire, and the glint of the lighthouse and the deep breathing of that beloved Baby in your bed."

It is all, she writes, because of the students he has to stay in Cork to examine, "a score of silly, snuffley, mean, conceited, irrepressible, unspeakable students [who] have to be met, seen, smelt, felt, borne with, shone upon, ploughed, passed, hustled, scorned, pitied, forgotten, and anything else beyond my vocabulary". Why, in this time of "heavenly weather", does he have to be "shut up" in his "mildewed halls of science", when he might be "crawling thro' brown bracken" with his "bare body" and "sleeping in the quarry on the warren on soft heather among rabbits and other creatures of the night ... Oh how odious is the present state of civilization and hateful are houses, clothes, servants, dust and animal food ... At least that's at this moment the feeling of your graminivorous savage woman."

A journalist described Kit Sandford as a "famous and attractive figure in Irish medicine ... equally expert on the tennis court, on the bank of a salmon reach, and on the deck of a yacht". He was also a contemplative individual, a man of books, and "such quiet pleasures, with those of travel in his later years, played a large part in his life". His marriage to Mary was "an ideal union" and for many years Kit and Mary were "the most sought-after couple in Cork".

This popularity, presumably, resulted in a photographic slide of their first-born, Christopher, my father, being projected for some years onto the screen of a Cork cinema, wearing his dressing-gown and holding a candle, to bring the evening show to an end.

IN 1910, when John was eighteen, Ralfe twelve, Christopher seven and Anthony five, a fire broke out in the attics of Castle Freke.

Kit, in Cork at the time, received a telegram telling him of the fire at eight in the morning and at once rang up the City Fire Brigade and the head of the Cork Brigade, Superintendent Hutson. The latter, according to the local newspaper, set out in "a powerful motor car", accompanied by a couple of firemen, a quarter of a mile of hose, "chemical engines", and John Carbery.

Kit and Mary followed in a second motor car. Cork police telegraphed those in Bandon and Clonakilty to clear the roads, so that within seventy-five minutes of setting out the party arrived at Castle Freke. As they approached the castle they realized it was doomed. Kit, to the alarm of his wife, braved smoke and flames to go down into the cellar where the family silver was stored. With relief he realized that the flames would not be able to penetrate the safe in which it was secured. On the way out he was "nearly killed" by falling masonry.

Late that night, when she and Kit got back to St Patrick's Place, Mary sat down to write to her friend Doty Bandon:

> It is with a heavy heart that I write to tell you of the destruction of dear Castle Freke. We saw the smoke from near Clonakilty and when we got there the house was blazing.
>
> It was so *grievous* watching the beautiful oak room burning and the organ – my sitting-room – Oh! Doty dear – I feel so *homeless*, and never again will it be *my* home, never shall I see *my* babies round the nursery table, for it will take 2 or 3 years, I should think, to rebuild. It is too sad, and I feel *broken*.
>
> John was quite *splendid* and came out wonderfully but, poor child, he is very sad tonight. All the poor "neighbours" were so

kind, everything was got into shelter and sorted. We have many mercies to be thankful for, and no lives were lost in the splendid fight made by our men against the flames.

Beginning in the roof, there was no chance of saving the house. I rather hoped you would drive over and yet I am glad you didn't, dear Doty, as it was a sad sight.

The castle was insured and Mary at once began to plan its rebuilding on the same grand scale (see Appendix), although some say that John, now a spirited young man of eighteen, was already adamant that he would rather she didn't. Some people claim he had some premonition of those events which, all too soon, were to rock Ireland and forever undermine the authority of those who, like the Carberys, believed themselves to be the backbone of Ireland.

Despite the castle being in ruins, the family continued to spend much of their time there, living in Kilkerran Cottage, which Mary had rebuilt and modernized.

In the summer of 1911, while the rest of the family were staying in the cottage, Mary and Ralfe went up to the castle to sleep in one of the towers that had been saved from the fire. Owls and bats and the sound of dripping rain made it "bogey".

Over the next few years the floors and roof of the castle were reconstructed in reinforced concrete, and steel window-frames were installed, in the hope that this would prevent fire from raging through it again. Craftsmen worked to provide plasterwork ceilings, panelling, elaborately carved chimney-pieces, and a huge oak staircase in Edwardian-Jacobean style.

WHILE WAITING for Castle Freke to be rebuilt, Mary indulged herself travelling in her horse-drawn caravan. From a common where they were parked near Llandindrod Wells, in Wales, her diary notes "an interesting talk" she'd had with a "Welsh nonconformist (a dear friend of Lloyd George)". Sitting in one of her collapsible chairs by the caravan, the Welshman told her that Lloyd George and many others "anticipate *revolution* in England, and are straining every nerve to prevent it". In Wales, said the nonconformist, the "educated workman" felt a terrible anger for "the idle rich (not those who do their duty)", and a "terrible feeling" against "the millionaire who motors all over the country, and eats and drinks and enjoys himself and thinks nothing of the poor". There was much to agree with in what he said, Mary decided.

By August 1912 the caravan was in Ballyvourney in West Cork. Kit was driving every day in his motor car to work in Cork and returning in the evening with provisions. One afternoon, in pouring rain, Mary and the children "got into the van and tied the horses behind, but 11 times Kingcup broke away and had to be caught and tied up again". Kit overtook them before dark and "rode Kingcup, leading Paddy, through torrents of rain, until at last we reached Macroom about 8.30, 25 miles". There they rang "boldly" at the "great gateway of the old Castle". Out came a "sort of a porter" who, recognizing Kit, invited them in enthusiastically. The caravan "squeezed through the most ancient gateway and anchored just inside under a great wall and a tree".

John Carbery did not come on these trips. Photographs from those days show him and his brother Ralfe standing with a certain hauteur, holding in their hands the instruments of animal slaughter – not that unusual for young men of the time.

About John's upbringing Mary had taken infinite trouble. She told me how she used to leave books open at interesting pages, hoping that his attention would be captured and that he would read on. Perhaps, however, she was too intrusive, giving him too little room to discover who he really was. By caring too much and being too "saintly" she achieved the opposite effect to that which she desired.

There were incidents that gave cause for alarm. One story begins with Mary reminding John that it is a very special saint's day on which all Christians everywhere try to be kind to animals. Later that day John said to my grandmother, "I was kind to animals. I was very kind."

"Oh, good, John, what did you do?"

"I gave the canary to the cat."

At the age of eight John lined up a gardener and shot an apple off his head with an air pistol. A hat he shot off an alarmed poacher in the castle demesne, slightly grazing his head, was shown – complete with bullet hole – to the present Lord Carbery on a recent visit.

In 1911 John, now nineteen, drove Kit, Mary and Connie the chauffeur on a tour through Germany and Austria. It was not a happy experience. Mary and Kit came back with "shattered nerves". Connie was relieved to be home, for "he felt sure he would be killed entirely".

At fourteen years of age John had gone secretly to Cork and arrived back driving his first motor car. Later he bought an aeroplane which he landed on the strand at Castle Freke. John was a charismatic young man around whom gossip accumulated. Winifred Gloster, a neighbour, describes how "The young Lord Carbery was a constant source of interest. The day War No. 1 started he arrived at Blackrock, near Cork, in the first aeroplane and caused quite a sensation." Much alarm was caused when some people assumed this was the start of a German invasion.

Another neighbour, Arthur Helps, tells how once on a visit to the deserted castle he was wandering around "thinking of the old times of its glory", when he "saw the picture of some Lord Carbery with his hounds, in which each animal had been shot in the eye with a .22 rifle". He heard other stories of things being shot, "including a donkey with children riding it, probably your father among them".

THE REBUILDING of Castle Freke was complete by 1913. Mary threw a "grand ball" to celebrate John's coming of age. There was also an "outside party": long tables, a pipe band, and a cartload of drink, mainly "Rassler" beer from Clonakilty.

A glittering marriage was what Mary had in mind for John, the scion of an ancient family who claimed to trace the male line back to the third century, a family who were cousins to the Cecils, the Wroughtons, the Bandons.

John took a different view. Within two weeks of the ball, he had married José Metcalfe, a spectacularly beautiful young woman. Her father, Major "Jumbo" Metcalfe, came from a military background and was a member of White's Club in London. He was also known for his extravagant gambling.

Debonair, wealthy, titled, brave, John for some years held the record for the Cresta Toboggan Run and represented Britain in the Schneider Trophy competition for the fastest plane on earth. He had met José while skiing at St Moritz. She and another woman there had found him especially desirable. They tossed a coin for him and José won. The Cresta Run was dangerous and José now set about winning John's heart by taking her place on the toboggan as part of an all-male team, an astonishing thing for a woman to do at that time. John admired courage and unconventionality in women, and fell in love with her.

EPILOGUE

JOSÉ was with John when, in July 1914, at the age of twenty-two, he gave an aeronautical exhibition over Cork and then landed his plane on the University athletic grounds. The *Cork Examiner* sets the scene:

> He took his seat in the machine. His mechanic turned the propellor and the engine went to work right away, its eight cylinders emitting an artillery-like roar. Immediately on the machine getting clear, Lord Carbery put the monoplane in motion and ran it a short distance when it ascended at a very narrow angle to the ground, so narrow indeed that the uninitiated (and most of those present were uninitiated) believed that it would go straight to the football posts.
>
> However, when about 30 yards from the posts, the aviator cleverly changed the steering of his machine giving it an extraordinary angle to the ground so much so that it was almost perpendicular. In this manner it ascended swiftly and sharply and still rising it headed off in a north westerly direction.

John Carbery gave other displays over Bandon and Clonakilty. "The people of the district," said one newspaper, would have "an opportunity of witnessing the daring and youthful aviator performing in the air feats which it would be impossible to describe, and must be seen to be believed". And it later reported that there were "shrieks and gasps of terror" when "the noble Lord looped the loop over the crowd".

Towards the end of the display, José went up in the plane with her husband. She was wearing a "tight-fitting dark cap". Although said by some to be looking rather pale, "she evidently enjoyed the prospect of looping the loop".

After the display at Clonakilty, John wrote to Monsignor O'Leary: "I would give my share of the gate receipts to the fund for forming a branch of the National Volunteers at Clonakilty. In politics I am personally a supporter of the policy of the Irish Party and absolutely dissociate myself from the Unionists."

John also took part in a flight from London to Paris and back with six other competitors. He was running second on the return leg when his plane came down on the sea. He was picked up by a steamer and eventually brought back to Britain by the battleship HMS *St Vincent*.

The businessmen of Clonakilty invited John to "have a drink with the town". There is a photograph of the event. All have a tipsy look about them and John, who as a baby had been "mobbed" in Skibbereen, is clearly now being given an alcoholic version of the freedom of the city.

On 12 July 1914 a public meeting was held in Clonakilty Town Hall to start up a branch of the Irish National Volunteers. Monsignor O'Leary presided. It was proposed that they call it The Lord Carbery Branch of the Irish National Volunteers. This was passed unanimously.

In the words of the *Cork Examiner*, "From Cork to Clon ... he was Lord of the skies." But John was about to lose much of his reputation. Few, outside his family, could have had an inkling at that time of his coming fall from grace.

IN AUGUST 1914 Britain was at war with Germany. In 1915 Mary went to stay with the Bandons and took Doty to visit Kilkerran Cottage and Castle Freke. The castle, she felt, had gone to "rack and ruin" since John and José had moved in. After having tea with Mrs Jenkins, the head gardener's wife, they ventured a "prowl about the garden" with "poor downhearted" Jenkins. "You never saw such a *deteriorated* garden," wrote Mary to her mother, "cabbages in the bowling green, hay on the grassy lawns, weeds everywhere. One can see there is no *heart* in the dear place."

At the bottom of this letter there is a sad scribbled later note: "After this visit the Lodgekeepers were ordered not to allow either Doty or me to go through."

Mary was no longer welcome at Castle Freke. She returned there before Christmas 1915 for her usual present-giving. The estate was closed to her but the local priest lent her a room in the Roman Catholic school.

MARY was in Cork at the time of the Easter Rising in 1916. From St Patrick's Place she wrote:

All is quiet here, but we are quite cut off from Dublin, the lines having been damaged ... Thank God that poor rebel Cork kept quiet and sane. All the Irish troops have been sent to England, it is said, and cavalry arrived here this morning and people say that the guns were rumbling in during the night ...

Kit eats nothing and is all nerves ... I feel more than ever like Mrs Elizabeth Freke! Perhaps I am her reincarnation!

From an English perspective the Irish struggle for independence was seen as "disloyalty" and was believed to have been stirred up by Germany. *The Times* leader of Wednesday 26 April described the "insane rising" as "evidently the result of a carefully arranged plot, concocted between the Irish traitors and their German confederates". This view brought an impassioned response from Mary's neighbour Edith Somerville, who, in the first and last letter she wrote to *The Times*, pleaded for clemency. It was English negligence, she believed, that had allowed the rise of Sinn Féin. She had heard of "more than one state-supported school" in remote parts of Munster in which "the greatness and generosity of Germany", and "the reptile villainy of England", were given as themes for essays by the students. As a result of this, she says, boys of nine or ten, "quick as ever to learn the romance of revolt", grew into "senseless, reckless, slaughtering idealists" dedicated to the "mad dream of Ireland a Nation".

Mary was convinced that, if the Germans succeeded in securing Ireland as an ally, they would quickly become tyrants and subjugate the country, turning the Irish people into virtual slaves. She wrote a series of satirical letters allegedly from "The Baron von Kartoffel" and others, which appeared in the correspondence columns of a Cork newspaper in 1916 and were then published anonymously in book form as "The Germans in Cork". The letters suppose that the Baron has been made Military Governor of Cork, and describe the town under German rule. The leaders of Sinn Féin have been told they are to be sent abroad: "They would have been no more loyal to us than they were to England [writes the Baron] ... But I cannot help pitying them – a little. They little know what is before them." In a painfully prophetic passage, the Baron also arranges for the gassing of the thousand inmates of the Cork lunatic asylum.

RALFE, aged twenty at the start of the war, fought in France and was later awarded the MBE. John enlisted, complete with his own aeroplane, in the Royal Naval Air Service. During the earlier part of the war he flew over the German trenches and lobbed bombs out of his cockpit. The end of the war did not bring to an end Mary's worries about John. Ralfe too was now becoming a cause for concern. The young men had acquired values different from those thought desirable by their mother. John, at the age of twenty-seven, already married and a father, and Ralfe at twenty-four, appear to have gone for good looks rather than "background" in their choice of female companions.

Mary had not been on speaking terms with John since his marriage, but in 1919, after much agonizing, she asked him and José to visit her, so that they could be reconciled. The meeting took place at Woolley Park in England, which she had borrowed from her cousins the Wroughtons. It went as well as could be hoped, and Mary felt she had done the right thing.

Two months later, however, she was horrified to hear that José had begun divorce proceedings against John. They had been living in Kenya and he had been whipping her. Friends of his, while admitting there had been a sjambok cattle-whip in the bedroom, explained that John was using it to get rid of a wild animal that had got in and that José was in the way.

It was not easy to get divorced in those days. The marriage was finally dissolved, on 2 July 1920, by act of parliament called "An Act to Dissolve the Marriage of José Baroness Carbery and John Baron Carbery of Castle Freke in the County of Cork"; the dissolution made headlines in the Irish and English press. In June 1913, according to the Act, John had given José a black eye. The alleged whipping in Kenya occurred in April 1918, causing "extreme pain and distress". Two months later, says the Act, he committed adultery for three nights running in a Paris hotel.

THE SEPARATION of John and José was not the only event of 1919 that Mary found distressful. It was also that year that John put Castle Freke up for sale. The house had formed the backdrop for many generations of ancestors. His mother and siblings loved it deeply. Great hardship was caused locally when so many workers on the estate and in the castle became unemployed.

How could he have done this? I have been told that José was snubbed by neighbours and did not fit well into the West Cork environment. Others claim that Mary had told neighbours that John and José did not want to be called on, and that as a result José was distressed, feeling she was being ostracized.

There were other possible factors. Ireland had emerged from the First World War straight into a war of its own against England. The Indian summer of the Ascendancy, which Mary had enjoyed up to 1914, was over. Sinn Féin, having won the post-war election, refused to wait for England to grant Ireland independence, or to accept the kind of Home

Rule envisaged by Lloyd George's government. The British retaliated by sending an army of "auxiliaries", the Black and Tans, to reinforce the police. Atrocity bred atrocity. Cork suffered particularly. Owners of country houses and of cattle, even those who were neutral or sympathetic to Irish independence, were caught between the opposing sides.

Many of the great Anglo-Irish houses and castles in County Cork were burned down at this time. Many Anglo-Irish families left, but many also stayed. Castle Freke was not burned down. John need not have gone.

MARY suffered in the moments of saying goodbye to Castle Freke. She wrote to my father:

> My "Deare Darling",
> I am at last gone from beloved Castle Freke. The week has been a nightmare of furious work from morn to night, pack, pack, pack, and then hurried drives in the twilight to say goodbye to one and another. The poor people *can't* believe we are gone for good – and oh! the crying and wailing, the furtive tears in *men's* eyes, the hand-kissing, it was all very touching and went to my heart. To love and to be loved is all that *matters* in life, especially the *first*.
>
> I left after tea yesterday – the sea silver and the sky primrose; a cold wind sending the spindrift flying. I came by Ounahincha, the motor brimful of boxes, parcels, lampshades, clocks, crockery, coats, sticks, rugs.
>
> It was so cold.

There were yet other events in 1919 which, from Mary's point of view, gave cause for alarm. "Oh give me the joys of the city," Ralfe was writing in his leather-bound "Book of things worth remembering", which he kept securely locked:

> The theatre and the dance,
> And girls in their low-necked dresses
> Who throw one a winning glance.

Mary felt that Ralfe was getting into dangerous company. He had been seen wining and dining and was said to be considering getting engaged to a young woman who both his mother and his grandmother Victoria believed to be "unsuitable".

> Let me have supper at Murrays
> With some little girl so sweet,
> Mingle among the dancers
> With swiftly moving feet.
> Give me the passion I long for
> That makes one feel so free,
> And some little girl to sup with
> The London night for me.

Mary had different views about the "London night", and so did Victoria. "I do trust our prayers are being answered for Ralfe," she wrote to Mary. "I think I had better write to him to tell him, when he returns, to be sure and put up at my house. I dread his return to where we cannot get at him in London. No boy of his age is safe in London, unless he is a sage." There is a postscript: "Sad news came to me by wire. Ralfe married at the Spanish Place Catholic Church today. *News confidential.*"

IN IRELAND, the violence continued. In June 1921 Doty Bandon, Mary's cousin by marriage, and her seventy-year-old husband were roused from sleep and ordered outside Castle Bernard. The raiders set fire to the castle and took away Lord Bandon. The local military garrison and fire engine arrived too late to put out the flames. The soldiers then rounded up a large number of men from the streets of Bandon and brought them to move out as much of the furniture and valuables as they could onto the lawn. A photograph of the time shows the lawn looking like a furniture shop and the castle ablaze behind.

Mary was in London at the time and "battled round to the Ladies Bandon to pick up some news". Louie Bernard told her that the Sinn Féiners broke open a box at Castle Bernard with the Bandons' coronation robes and coronet in it, and "one strutted about the house with the coronet! They were very rude and rough and wouldn't let Doty dress and kept saying dreadful things."

Lord Bandon was held hostage while Sinn Féin leaders discussed peace terms with the British authorities in Dublin. On 11 July a truce was called and he was returned the next day to Castle Bernard. He found the sight of his ruined house unbearable and went on to Cork and thence to London.

Kit Sandford's country house overlooking Cork was a casualty of the Civil War which followed the Anglo-Irish Treaty. In 1922 the house was occupied by anti-Treaty forces who planted a bomb by the front door when they retreated. A herdsman detonated the bomb before the Free State army arrived. The house was later rebuilt with only one storey in front. It is now a golf club. Marks of shrapnel are still to be seen on the pillars of its elegant porch.

MARY AND KIT, once the Castle Freke days were over, wandered through much of Europe. Kit still spent time in Ireland continuing his duties, but apart from that they lived elsewhere in a series of rented houses and hotels. Mary's restlessness led them to Cray, Auchnacree, Avening, Woolley in Berkshire, Fontainbleau, Jura, St Arnoult, Doucier, Bovey, Majorca, Mürren; they never spent more than a few months in any one place. She was interested in the Gypsy culture and language, and believed that her frequent journeys by means of carriages, boats, trains, cars, and in her own custom-built caravan, reflected the Gypsy side of her nature. The caravan was sometimes sent on ahead by barge or train. Mary travelled long distances in it, at one point crossing the Simplon Pass in Switzerland, pulled by white oxen. The caravan incorporated inventions of her own – a collapsible canvas basin for washing, stackable metal beds and a tin bath made accessible by raising part of the floor. Creeping Jenny hung down from window-boxes at the back and "Creeping Jenny" was the name inscribed on the front of the caravan. It was from the windows of this caravan that my father first saw the Welsh border country of Shropshire and Herefordshire, which he was later to make his home.

Mary's wanderlust had been shared by Algy; they had wandered the world while they were together, and it may have been the wanderer in him that made him go on that last reckless journey to die in a hotel in Malvern, rather than spend his last days in his tent on the lawn at Castle Freke.

Kit, though he tended to fall in with most of Mary's plans, would have preferred a quieter life. Living in so many hotels and rented houses exhausted him. He would rather have been in his own house, walking the dogs and doing odd jobs about the place.

"Just as I am by nature restless, a mover on, so do I want to grow, and mentally to progress; to have a wider horizon, to 'cross the ranges'," wrote Mary. It was a fine philosophy but one which, freed of the duties of rearing a family, and of the anchor of Castle Freke, made her a demanding companion.

MARY'S INTEREST in Irish folklore and local history remained strong even after she left Castle Freke. At the start of her book *The Farm by Lough Gur* she relates how "In the summer of 1904 I was in the county Limerick seeking the words of a lost song. In the little town of Bruff, where the song was born, Mrs Fogarty welcomed me to her home on the bank of the lovely river Dawn, or Morning Star." Mary Carbery found in Mary Fogarty, whom she had first met in 1901, an enthusiast for the old stories and legends of Lough Gur. "She told me about the notable banshee Ainë and her brother Fer Fi, the dwarf; fairies in the hollow hills; a drowned city in the Enchanted Lake; giants and ghosts, saints' wells and fairy thorns. She had even in her youth heard the lost song sung."

An extensive correspondence developed. While Mary Fogarty, in east Limerick, remembered and made notes, Mary Carbery, in England, was weaving the reminiscences, as she received them, into a "continuous narrative". Here and there she filled gaps "which memory gave in shadowy form, or withheld" with material of her own gleaned from history, folklore and other sources. She wrote:

> ... by long thinking and dwelling on the past, by talking and by answering questions put to her, the mist cleared, and her awakened memory gave back in startling clarity scenes from the past – places, people and events, even fragments of conversation. She saw with the eyes of her mind her parents in their vigour, her nurse, the dairymaids, farm labourers, horses and dogs; once more she worked and played with her sisters, was dutiful to visiting aunts, answered the greetings of wayfarers who came to the door and received their blessings when they passed on their way.

The result was *The Farm by Lough Gur*, published in 1937, a book still well known in Ireland. Ireland had given wonderful things to Mary, and in *The Farm by Lough Gur* she gave a gift in return. It is a piece of social history, the story of a family of Catholic "strong farmers" in the nineteenth century. Mary presented, in the words of Shane Leslie's introduction to the book, "all the mists and memories, all the scent and sting of the Irish countryside". It is still in print fifty years after her death.

MY FATHER CHRISTOPHER showed great reticence about his half-brother John. Often he would decline to comment at all. He had been unhappy at school, and as a boy and young man Castle Freke represented the best of everything he knew. John had sold it out of the family, and he found it hard to forgive this.

Along with many other Irish people, John had developed a hatred for England, which he called "Johnny Bull". This may have been the reason that in 1921 he stopped using his title and assumed by deed poll the name John Evans Carberry. After some practice he began to speak in a broad American accent, which he used for the rest of his life.

In 1920 John had bought an estate in Kenya, called Seremai, "the place of death", and the scene of an ancient battle. His second wife, Maia, was one of a number of early women pilots in Kenya in the mid-twenties. They had one child, Juanita. Maia died in 1928 in a flying accident, when Juanita was still quite young. Juanita lived on at Seremai, though later she was to spend long periods away at eight different boarding-schools.

John married a third time. His new wife, the beautiful, streetwise June Weir Mosley of Johannesburg, was the only woman in his life able to withstand his wild behaviour. Soon after they met John took her up in a plane and asked if she would like to do some stunts. To show she wasn't afraid, June undid her safety-belt. John admired courage, and the gesture won his deep affection. She was described later to me as a "terrifyingly unnatural blonde. Deep bass voice. Tough as boots. But a wonderful person, warm-hearted and totally unjealous. Cut her in half, you'd find mostly gin."

John and June had violent rows, but he adored her. She had several affairs, aided and abetted by a governess John had engaged for Juanita. John usually didn't mind. Once, however, when June went off with a lover on a trip to Meru while John was away in his aeroplane, he came back unexpectedly. When he discovered his wife gone, he took off again and flew until, far below him, he caught sight of the couple driving across a desolate area. He had loaded the plane with medium-sized boulders, with which he bombarded their car. One of John's lesser-known projects was the financing of Beryl Markham's attempt to fly non-stop from England to New York, a flight not yet successfully done solo.

John's servants called him "Msharisha", the Kikuyu name for the long whip with which oxen are driven, because he lashed them frequently. At a wedding party at the White Rhino Hotel at Nyeri, soon after the outbreak of the Second World War, he proposed the toast, "Long live Germany. To hell with England." He was reported to the police, but the matter went no further.

In due course he spent a period in prison for contravening "Defence Regulations" with "currency offences". Initially sentenced to three years' hard labour, he appealed to the Supreme Court in Nairobi and the sentence was reduced to one year's simple imprisonment. He later referred to his time in gaol as "the happiest period of my life".

John and June also became involved in the furore that followed the murder in January 1941 of Josslyn Hay, Lord Erroll, who was found dead on the floor of his Buick, near Nairobi, with a bullet in his head. Sir "Jock" Delves Broughton, another member of the "Happy Valley set", is generally believed to have killed him. His wife Diana was beautiful, younger than him, and a close friend of June's. Diana had fallen in love with Erroll and was having an affair with him. June had been with them on the night of the murder and appeared as a defence witness.

The day after the murder Jock confessed to Juanita, then aged fifteen, that he had killed Lord Erroll; in her autograph book that day he wrote that his greatest love was "animals" and his greatest fear "loneliness". It was difficult for the young Juanita to live with this secret, and when she tried to share it with her stepmother she was beaten. She was called as a prosecution witness at the trial but discharged as unreliable. Jock Broughton was acquitted. He returned to Britain and killed himself, in the Adelphi Hotel, soon after his boat arrived at Liverpool. Juanita says this was not primarily because of the Erroll murder case, but because he had been accused of an insurance fraud relating to some pearls.

Juanita now lives in London and I recently asked her whether the beatings she received from her father – as documented in *White Mischief*, James Fox's account of the Erroll murder and the colonial demi-monde in Kenya – had been exaggerated. "Not at all," she said, and showed me, hanging on the wall, the rhino-hide whip her father had used.

With the collapse of the semi-feudal life of the old Anglo-Irish estates, and the growing independence of Ireland from what was seen as British imperialism, the likes of John had been born into a generation for whom there was no obvious role any more. Mary failed to understand this, thinking that after the war things would go back to normal.

John seldom returned to Ireland. In West Cork he is remembered as a brave aeronaut and as a courageous man who, for a few years during the Troubles, flew from the battlements of Castle Freke the tricoloured flag of an independent Ireland.

JOHN AND RALFE, and the loss of Castle Freke, broke Mary's heart. But she had one son for whom she felt her methods of upbringing had worked. This was Christopher, my father, born in 1902.

Feeling that he did not wish to return to Ireland once his brother had sold Castle Freke, my father in the thirties acquired Eye Manor, a fine Restoration house in the Welsh border country which, during his later years, he opened to the public.

Christopher had founded the Boar's Head Press and became owner and director of the Golden Cockerel Press, which he ran for many years. "We meditate upon the form that the book should be made to assume. During the months, and sometimes years, of our labour ... we have always the image we conceived for it before our eyes," he wrote of his publishing.

The Cockerel books were sumptuous: printed on vellum or handmade paper; often bound in pigskin or morocco, illustrated by carefully chosen artists, printed in beautiful historic typefaces. Even in the thirties books from the Golden Cockerel Press sold for up to one hundred guineas each, although my father also turned out small and exquisite books for as little as two shillings and sixpence.

It was in a cottage in the grounds of Eye Manor that Mary Carbery spent the last decade of her life. During the Second World War and in the austere period that followed, the lawns were not mown, and my father's horses grazed them because every bit of turf must "do its bit". Along once-decorative borders a gardener was now planting potatoes, "digging for victory". Nonetheless, the clean lines of the William and Mary mansion, the weeping ash, the gnarled and lichened trees in the orchards whose apples we shook down in autumn to be sent to the cider factory at Bulmers, and the unlikely horse-drawn caravan, constituted an environment in which Grandmother was contented.

She lived in a Virginia creeper-covered cottage with her "companion"

Sophie. Both of them wore whalebone stays which creaked when they moved, and both were deaf. Of an afternoon my grandmother would sit in her wheelchair under a yew tree, with Sophie on a hard-backed wooden chair beside though slightly behind her. They held shouted conversations, punctuated by long gaps, pointing large black bakelite ear trumpets at each other to pick up each other's remarks.

Mary and Sophie regularly attended services in the church that lay across the lawn. Grandmother told me that at her funeral she wanted nothing to do with the soft tones of dulcet or dulciana or *lieb gedacht*: "Pull out the trumpet-stop," she cried, "and let the organ peal in triumph for the arrival of one more soul into the realms of light!"

WE CHILDREN would approach Mary's two austere rooms on the first floor of her cottage through the dark and cavernous downstairs room where Sophie presided over a black stove that never went out. Narrow uncarpeted stairs led up to Grandmother.

Grandmother took our education seriously, instructing us in many subjects by means of daily lessons. She had invented various unusual ways of teaching mathematics and grammar which she tried out on my sisters. Being older and already at school, I escaped the worst of this. *The Pilgrim's Progress* was her favourite book and another teaching device was a peepshow with scenes from that story that she'd constructed herself, to be shown in the dark, lit by a torch which could be changed from white to red or green.

Austerity and simplicity were imposed on our lives by the war and the post-war years. In Mary's case this was increased by her own fastidiousness. There were bare boards under the high iron bed where she passed much of her time, and a very small fire burned in the narrow grate of the other upstairs room which was her living-room. Eggs were in short supply but, despite this, she never ate the yolks but only the whites.

Mary died in 1949 and her ashes were buried next to Kit's in the churchyard at Eye. A small plaque on the wall closest to Eye Manor bears the names of Mary, Kit, and my mother and father, whose ashes are also buried there.

WINDSWEPT CROACHNA HILL, just over the rise from Castle Freke, faces out towards the Atlantic and the sunset, as well as the mystic isle of

Moy Mell, and a dangerous submerged rock of the same name. Here, in 1901, in view of the countless sailors who would pass and re-pass through the years, Grandmother had caused to be erected a huge cross as a monument to her first husband Algy, the last Carbery to spend his life in these parts and to make his home in County Cork. It is visible from the Fastnet to the west almost to the Old Head to the east.

There was a time when the famous Cross of Monasterboice held the record for weight and height in Ireland but the Great Cross of Carbery exceeds it. Fourteen tons of white limestone rise thirty feet into the sky. There are seven panels, each with sculptured designs from the Bible. The inscription on the east face reads: "To the greater glory of God, and in loving memory of Algernon William George, 9th Baron Carbery, who was born 9th September 1868 and who died 12th June 1898. This Cross has been erected by Mary, his wife, 1901. The souls of the righteous are in the hand of God, they are in peace."

The east side contains a sculptured crucifixion and biblical scenes in which the women have a grace but the men, to modern eyes, can be felt to suffer from that rather wet look that can be the result of an overdose of piety. The rest of the cross is extensively decorated with traditional Irish motifs. It is impressive, even though now partly obscured by a large water storage reservoir which has been placed between it and the sea, and the whole area, on the day I visited, had a strong odour from the slurry that had been laid on the field in front of it.

Tradition has it that Algy was cremated and that his ashes rest beneath the cross in a casket of gold. Tradition also says that many have dug round the cross to try to find the casket, without success.

Half a mile or so away stands Castle Freke. In 1919 it was bought by a local consortium who planned to sell it to the singer John McCormack, but were unsuccessful. For many decades it survived almost intact, let to a Catholic religious organization. It was occupied by the Irish army during the Emergency. Then in the 1950s the house was gutted. Everything that could be removed – staircase, panelling, electric light-fittings, balustrade – was sold in an auction. Castle Freke once again became a ruin.

Close to the cross also stand the ruins of the family seat of worship, Rathbarry Church. In 1896 Mary and Algy placed "a fine stained-glass window" in the chancel, and encaustic tiling with big Art Nouveau lettering saying "Till He Comes", as well as a Holy Table of carved oak, chancel rails, a lectern and font, a mural monument to John, the 6th Baron, and a new organ dedicated to Algy's father. Most of these have gone, but the graves for servants and the vast family mausoleum are there still.

Mary's grave is not there, but she often told me that her heart would remain on the windswept shores of West Cork, at Castle Freke.

APPENDIX

Sale Particulars of Castle Freke, July 24th 1919

By direction of The Right Honourable Lord Carbery

IRELAND

The
Marine, Residential and Sporting Domain
known as

CASTLE FREKE
County Cork

Extending to about 1,100 ACRES
Shooting, Fishing, Yacht Anchorage

Castle Freke occupies a charming position, facing South, overlooking the undulating, well-timbered park to the Sea. The greater part of Castle Freke was burned down some eight years ago and this was rebuilt at a very heavy outlay – the interior of reinforced concrete – thus being fireproof, and it now enjoys all modern comforts and conveniences. It contains Large Vestibule, Spacious Saloon, Drawing Room, Music Room, Dining Room,

Smoking Room, 21 Bedrooms, 3 Dressing Rooms, Day and Night Nurseries, 4 Bath Rooms, 9 Men Servants' Bedrooms, Ample Domestic Offices. Electric Light, Central Heating, Modern Drainage.

The Gardens and Grounds surrounding Castle Freke are undulating, well timbered and of great natural beauty. Shady walks to Promontories above the Sea. Woodland Walks, Terraced Lawns, Tennis Courts, Rose and Carnation Gardens, Prolific Walled Kitchen Gardens.

Stabling – Accommodation for 14 horses, Coach house, Garage; 8 rooms for men. *Home Farm* with ample buildings. *Three Lodges* and 9 cottages.

Sport – Good mixed shooting, including Wild Duck, Snipe, Woodcock and Pheasants. *Hunting* with the Carbery, Bandon and Cork Foxhounds.

Deep Sea Fishing – Trout Fishing in Lake Kilkerran. Bathing. Yacht Anchorage. Golf at Clonakilty.

Post and Telegraph Office at Castle Freke.

[Murky photographs illustrate the large brochure: 'ONE OF THE LODGES', 'A PORTION OF THE DRIVE', 'A WATERFALL IN THE GROUNDS', 'THE BEECH HEDGE'. Others show the battlemented and betowered castle itself, the Rathbarry ruins, and a couple of the rooms, ornate and crammed with paintings and furniture.]

The Castle is beautifully placed upon a terrace, facing South, commanding magnificent views over the undulating part to the Atlantic. It is approached along three beautiful Avenues, each with Lodge at entrance. It is entered through a pair of Studded Oak Doors, and the accommodation, which is conveniently arranged, comprises:

Stone Entrance Hall
with Cloak Recess and Lavatory. A flight of broad stone stairs leads to the Principal Floor, on which are:

The Vestibule
measuring 31 feet by 21 feet

The Saloon or Inner Hall
measuring 75 feet by 30 feet, with large open fireplace.
Amongst other rooms on the ground floor are:

The Drawing Room
measuring 33 feet by 24 feet, fitted with handsome oak mantel and handsome plaster ceiling, communicating with

The Music Room
measuring 48 feet by 21 feet, with oak beamed ceiling, oak mantel
and fitted oak bookcases, leading to

The Dining Room
measuring 33 feet by 21 feet, with carved oak mantel, oak beamed
ceiling and service door.

The Smoking Room
measuring 21 feet by 15 feet; one side is fitted with walnut enclosed
bookcase with shelves and drawers; tiled hearth and dog stove.

[These Reception Rooms, the brochure claims, have "glorious views over
undulating well-timbered park land" to "the rugged coast and Atlantic".
Their oak floors, "heated with hot water coils ... are very lofty and light".
What these days might be referred to as the Kitchen Wing is described:]

The Culinary Offices
are light, lofty and well arranged, and include KITCHEN, 30 feet by 21,
with Eagle range, roaster and sink; large SCULLERY, with three sinks,
SERVANTS' HALL; HOUSEKEEPER'S ROOM; BUTLER'S PANTRY, with
Strong Room, 12 feet by 6, Chubb's sink (hot & cold), fitted cupboards;
HOUSEMAID'S ROOM, with range, linen cupboards and sink (hot &
cold); BUTLER'S BEDROOM; Heating Room, with separate boilers for
house and bath; Larders; Wine Cellar; Store Rooms; Coal Cellars, etc.

There is a LIFT to the top of the house.

A Flat Roof
of reinforced concrete covered with asphalt, which is quite a good
surface for roller skating. Electric light is laid on.

THE DRAINAGE
was renewed throughout a few years ago, and no expense was spared
to bring it into perfect order.

THE WATER SUPPLY
is by gravitation, and is ample.

THE ELECTRIC LIGHT
is generated on the Farm and is conveyed to the Castle by an
underground cable.

Stone-built Lecture Hall
measuring about 35 feet by 17 feet, and fitted with Range.

There is the Home Farm, a largish number of cottages, and

Good Mixed Shooting

During the War no birds have been reared, and no bags have been kept, but a Purchaser might reasonably expect to obtain, during an average season, 300 Wild Ducks, 750 Snipe, 750 Woodcock, 500 Pheasants, besides a great number of Rabbits.

There is a KEEPER'S COTTAGE containing one Sitting Room, Three Bedrooms, and Kitchen.

Yachting and Fishing

There is Yacht Anchorage at Ross Bar, the adjoining Bay, whilst at Glandore, some five miles distant, a 1,000 ton Yacht could anchor and lie up for the winter. There is good Deep Sea Fishing, whilst KILKERRAN LAKE, half of which belongs to this Estate, provides good Trout Fishing.

SAFE SEA BATHING

The Gardens and Grounds

are undulating, delightfully timbered, and of great natural beauty. There are BROAD TERRACED LAWNS, whilst the many beautiful Woodland Walks form a charming feature of the Property. The ROSE GARDEN and the YOUNG ORCHARD are surrounded by a Beech Hedge about 12 feet high. The CARNATION GARDEN is protected on two sides by high stone walls covered with Wisteria, Magnolia, Abelia, Solanum and Jessamine.

There are many remarkably fine specimen Dracaene Trees, beautiful Eucalyptus Trees, whilst an enormous Fig Tree, whose boughs extend to some 60 feet, is probably the finest specimen in Great Britain. Beautiful Flowering Shrubs. Magnificent clumps of Rhododendrons. The HARD TENNIS COURT is protected on two sides by high walls, whilst the bluff rise of Copse-clothed Hills further shelters it. ANCIENT FLAG TOWER.

The THREE KITCHEN GARDENS are surrounded by walls, some 15–20 feet high, upon which grow, in great profusion, Plums, Pears & Peaches.

Peach House, Two Hot-houses. Potting Shed. Apple House.

GARDENER'S COTTAGE containing Sitting Room, Kitchen, Scullery, and Three Bedrooms.

PONY STABLING

The Gardens have an ample supply of water.

There is a very INTERESTING ANCIENT RUIN, formerly known as RATHBARRY CASTLE, once a fortified Redoubt.